NEW DIRECTIONS
FOR
PHILANTHROPIC
FUNDRAISING

Robert E. Fogal
Ohio Presbyterian Retirement Services Foundation
Dwight F. Burlingame
Indiana University Center on Philanthropy
EDITORS

CULTURES OF GIVING II

HOW HERITAGE, GENDER, WEALTH, AND VALUES INFLUENCE PHILANTHROPY

Charles H. Hamilton
J. M. Kaplan Fund
Warren F. Ilchman
Indiana University Center on Philanthropy

EDITORS

T0340139

NUMBER 8, SUMMER 1995

CULTURES OF GIVING II: HOW HERITAGE, GENDER, WEALTH, AND VALUES
INFLUENCE PHILANTHROPY
Charles H. Hamilton, Warren F. Ilchman (eds.)
New Directions for Philanthropic Fundraising, No. 8, Summer 1995
Robert E. Fogal, Dwight F. Burlingame, Editors

Microfilm copies of issues and articles are available in 16 mm and 35 mm, as well as
microfiche in 105 mm, through University Microfilms Inc., 300 North Zeeb Road,
Ann Arbor, Michigan 48106-1346.

ISSN 1072-172X   ISBN 0-7879-9951-2

NEW DIRECTIONS FOR PHILANTHROPIC FUNDRAISING is part of The Jossey-Bass
Nonprofit Sector Series and is published quarterly by Jossey-Bass Inc., Publishers,
350 Sansome Street, San Francisco, California 94104-1342.

SUBSCRIPTIONS: Please see Ordering Information at back of book.

EDITORIAL CORRESPONDENCE should be sent to Robert E. Fogal,
Ohio Presbyterian Retirement Services Foundation, OMNI Plaza,
4502 Darrow Rd., Rte. 91, Stow, OH 44224-1887.

Contents

Editors' Notes

THIS IS our second issue devoted to what we know about the "cultures of giving." Our objective is simple: we wish to assess the productivity of knowledge of choice—the choice of giving, the choice of improving odds in successfully asking. Is there anything that we, as social analysts and thoughtful practitioners, might know about different populations that would assist us or others in raising funds for philanthropic purposes—not to buy soap or bourbon, but to give to a college, a homeless shelter, or a symphony orchestra?

The word *assist* is important. Knowledge, like any resource, can be more or less productive, might reduce the "costs" of fundraising or increase the "yield." Professional conferences, formal instruction in fundraising, and journals such as this one aim to reduce the cost of learning what might be useful to achieve one's ends. We see in these two issues of *New Directions for Philanthropic Fundraising* a series of hypotheses about giving behaviors of different populations. We now have the opportunity to test in action the "truth quality" or practical applicability of these propositions.

The individuals who are the most informed in a factual sense may not be the most knowledgeable, and there is no linear relationship between knowing and being wise. It is appropriate then to ask, What have we accomplished with publication of these seventeen pieces? Do they provide helpful information? Do they add to our understanding and knowledge about giving? Finally, do they help us become wiser and more sensitive to some of the big issues that affect philanthropy and society at large?

Dividing the world into different categories for explanatory purposes can be done along various lines. Political or economic systems, religious preference, ethnicity, the role of women, and so forth can be used and tested to see whether we can explain differences in the behavior of giving. For example, the reductionist economic model

NEW DIRECTIONS FOR PHILANTHROPIC FUNDRAISING, NO. 8, SUMMER 1995 © JOSSEY-BASS PUBLISHERS

is often used to explain generous behavior. Analysts pursuing this form of explanation find the relative outcome of the transaction as difference enough to explain behavior. We think there is more to it than that. Indeed, in a world of multiple influences, the differences will always be "multivariable."

From the most abstract generalization to the most particular anecdotal example, the predictive quality of hypotheses rise and fall. It is sometimes argued that what we know least we attribute to "culture," and what we know most intimately we attribute to "personality." Nothing is more valuable than knowing your donor well. But are there guides in the search for donors and successful fundraising that are less time and resource consuming and more predictive of results? From the most abstract to the most specific, we would argue that there is comparative power to the values and behaviors—considered coherently as a "culture"—associated with individuals defined by a "common difference." The average or modal behavior of those so identified can then be tested by seeing in action whether the behavior can be predicted by the attribute (or, to save the research enterprise, whether the particular case is on the tail ends of the distribution and hence considered an explainable exception).

So with philanthropy and charity—giving and serving beyond the family. We could have analyzed a universal propensity such as a presumed generous gene and tried to see contemporary manifestations of giving. Where would that have gotten us? Instead, by breaking all humankind into smaller groups—gender, education, religious preference, ethnicity or race, region, kind of work, motivational values—we use that "difference" and giving behavior as a potentially predictive tool that can assist fundraisers in increasing the value of their efforts. At least, we hope so.

Each of these two issues on "cultures of giving" have tackled a number of these differences. Time and length considerations have limited what could be explored and the detail possible, thus many important issues and differences that deserve exploration must be left to other venues. These chapters can get us all started.

Region. In the first issue, Julian Wolpert and Rikki Abzug both write that region is still an important influence on charitable behavior. Local difference can be seen in the makeup of nonprofit boards of directors. Fundraising strategy needs to take this diversity into account.

Religion. Six authors explore religion in the first issue (Dean Hoge with a denominational overview, Daniel Conway on Stewardship, Calvin Pressley on the Black church, Anita Plotinsky on Jewish giving, James Hudnut-Beumler on Protestant giving, and Wesley Willmer on evangelical giving). Common challenges, different institutional structures, and variations in values all indicate that religious belief is an important determinate of giving.

Ethnic heritage. A large part of this second issue is devoted to ethnicity, following the contemporary search for such explanations. Four authors suggest a series of issues. Black giving is discussed by Jean Fairfax, Latino philanthropy is looked at by Michael Cortés, Stella Shao discusses Asian American giving, and Barry Kosmin looks at Jewish philanthropy. The tensions between separateness and assimilation are apparent in each article. The values and approaches to giving also point out both a universality of giving and great particularity. There are many suggestions for fundraising practice and practical testing.

Gender. Susan A. Ostrander and Joan M. Fisher suggest that the qualities and priorities often historically associated with women are good for philanthropy overall. An earlier issue of *New Directions for Philanthropic Fundraising* was devoted to this issue, and there are many testable propositions that practitioners and scholars need to explore further.

Motivation. We suspected that there were motivational imperatives that also move donors to give. These crosscut the other "differences" discussed above. We asked several authors to look at difference in this way in this issue. Paul G. Schervish and John J. Havens provide useful ideas about generosity from the standpoint of income and wealth, with important practical implications for fundraising. E. Gil Clary and Mark Snyder apply research on motivations for volunteering to giving behavior. Russ Alan Prince and Karen Maru File present their Seven Faces framework for looking at major donor groups by the motivations, values, and beliefs they share. Both of these two chapters present a number of personal and social motives, needs, and goals that may underlie giving decisions. Finally, Charles L. Eastman looks at how generational issues may explain quite a lot about differences in donor behavior.

Many of these chapters contain testable propositions or decision rules for action that seem obvious. And yet the jury is still out on the question of whether expert sense derived from "information" is superior to the "wisdom" of common sense. Some people seem to think scholarly pursuits are infallible. The problem lies less with the scholarship and more with the unseemly tendency of people to act differently than predicted. On the other hand, perhaps the best, most testable propositions arise out of experience of concrete situation, embellished by anecdotes and war stories. Perhaps there is no systematic knowledge that can aid judgment. We personally do not think that is the case. A combination of idea and action is the best way to promote philanthropy that is ethical and productive.

There is much yet to be known that might enhance the productivity of acting on knowledge of giving. These chapters can only scratch the surface. For instance, for all the differences, there should be a better sense of the margin—what additional inducement will increase the likelihood of giving. In addition, there needs to be a more intimate sense of which values the people characterized by the differences feel motivated to support: it is unlikely that African Americans can ever be persuaded to give to the Michigan Militia or the Aryan Nation. Finally, what of the fact that each of these articles notes a celebration of the charitable impulse of one sort or another?

From most of the papers here, we end up with the certain knowledge that people with resources give to missions they wish to see realized. Purpose and wherewithal seem to be the best initial explanatory values. But as scholars, practitioners, and citizens, we want more. Within different ethnic and religious communities, different genders, age cohorts, and so forth, the missions that count are nested. Knowing one without the other—purpose without wherewithal and wherewithal without purpose—is not knowledge for hire, to be put at the service of any objective by a fundraiser armed with such knowledge.

There is the need to see giving—the whole process that goes into fundraising—as a test of hypotheses and a feedback to their truth quality. If more fundraisers saw their work as tests of hypotheses or propositions, then we could all join together as scholars and practitioners to build a testable knowledge base. While the most knowledgeable fundraiser might not be the wisest, the most knowledgeable may be on the journey to understanding. It is to move us along in this journey that the findings here are presented. With these benchmarks as points of departure in an ongoing collaboration between scholars and practitioners, we are at least moving in the right direction.

Charles H. Hamilton
Warren F. Ilchman
Editors

CHARLES H. HAMILTON *is director of the J.M. Kaplan Fund, a New York City–based foundation. He is also a research associate at the Indiana University Center on Philanthropy and a visiting fellow at Yale University's Program on Non-Profit Organizations.*

WARREN F. ILCHMAN *is executive director of the Indiana University Center on Philanthropy and professor of philanthropic studies and public policy. Formerly professor at the University of California, he was program adviser to the Ford Foundation's International Division, dean of Boston University, provost and director of the Rockefeller College of Public Affairs and the Rockefeller Institute of Government, SUNY, and president of Pratt Institute. He is the author of twelve books.*

Part One

Heritage and philanthropy

*The potential for black philanthropy is remarkable
but accomplishing that potential requires two things:
first, we must understand the basic beliefs and the
dramatic history of black Americans and second,
we must actively engage all elements of the African
American community in defining, supporting, and
controlling their philanthropic future.*

1

Black philanthropy:
Its heritage and its future

Jean E. Fairfax

UNDERSTANDING two centuries of African American philanthropy
is central to understanding the black experience in America. Black
philanthropy is rooted in what James A. Joseph has called the
African cosmology of connectedness. In his address at the inaugu-
ration of the Association of Black Foundation Executives' James A.
Joseph Lecture Series in 1991, he stated: "The communal tradition
of caring for each other has deep historical and metaphysical roots.
Homo communalis, the idea that we live and have our being in a caring social community, is at the heart of African metaphysics. . . .
This cosmology of connectedness provided the first principle of
early black philanthropy" (pp. 4–5).

Since the eighteenth century, black philanthropy has been shaped
by the realities of life on this continent, that is, often the harsh reality
of oppression. As needs and challenges have changed, new forms of

NEW DIRECTIONS FOR PHILANTHROPIC FUNDRAISING, NO. 8, SUMMER 1995 © JOSSEY-BASS PUBLISHERS

organized philanthropy have evolved. But the philosophical roots have not withered. The concept of philanthropy as a communal enterprise, a manifestation of a community whose members care for one another, has remained in sharp contrast to the concept of philanthropy as noblesse oblige or the responsibility of the rich to provide charity to the deserving poor. In the annals of American philanthropy, according to Joseph, the "real heroes were the ordinary people who, with meager resources, accomplished extraordinary deeds. Mired in poverty, racked by frequent epidemics, and oppressed by vicious racism, the poor reached out to the poor, sharing what little they had with each other" (p. 7).

Black philanthropy has been a demonstration of solidarity with the oppressed. It has been a mechanism for survival, mutual assistance, and self-help, for social protest, for the struggle for justice, for the enhancement of the educational and economic status of blacks, and for the establishment of institutions.

Like Joseph, Emmett D. Carson, preeminent scholar of black philanthropy, has urged a larger context for understanding the African American culture of giving, one that includes the duality of black life, which is both African and American. This dual culture has driven black philanthropy, in its personal as well as its organized forms, into different directions from those of white efforts.

Early African American philanthropy

The number of examples of early African American philanthropy is impressive. A monograph by Frances L. Cudjoe, "Traditions of African-American Philanthropy in Boston" offers valuable information about historical Boston. The Fraternal Order of Prince Hall Masons, founded in 1775, provided mutual aid to freed slaves and their families; the order continues today as a national agency for service and scholarships. Social services, financial help, and job placement were available through the African Society for Mutual Aid and Charity, formed in 1796. The African-American Female Intelligence

Society, created in 1832, provided many services, including health insurance. The Juvenile Garrison Independent Society, active in the 1830s and 1840s as an organization for teenagers, sponsored fix-up projects and antislavery rallies. The Home for Aged Colored Women, designed in the 1860s to address the plight of elderly black women, still exists today. Renamed the Grimes-King Foundation, it is an advocate for their health and housing needs.

The African American culture of giving—its motivations, style, and scope—was also embodied in Philadelphia. By 1838, there were a hundred mutual aid societies in that city. The Free African Society was founded there in 1787 after its leaders were forcibly removed from a white church while praying. Spiritually rooted, autonomous, proudly African American, and committed to solidarity, service, and social activism, it assured a central role for the black church as a trusted black-controlled vehicle for philanthropy through coming generations. Like other black charitable groups there and elsewhere, it was actively involved in antislavery movements and the Underground Railroad, providing sanctuary and financial aid to runaway slaves. The Free African Society's volunteer service to white victims during Philadelphia's devastating plague of 1793 is especially remarkable because the leaders involved were the very same men who had been evicted from the white church. During the inaugural lecture mentioned at the beginning of this chapter, Joseph recounted this moving event:

The elders of the African Society met on September 5 and decided that they must see what the Negro inhabitants could do to help the stricken white citizens.

Two by two, they set out on a tour of the city. Absalom Jones and Richard Allen . . . visited more than twenty white families. Other Negroes did likewise, and afterwards all the elders came together again to tell what they had seen.

Next day Jones and Allen called on Mayor Clarkson to ask how the Negroes could be of most use. The mayor received them gratefully. . . . Most of his Federalist friends had fled, and nearly his entire civil service, but the city was at last producing new and courageous leaders from his humblest people. [p. 6]

Thus charity was not limited to members of the African American community; it even reached out to whites in distress in those communities where blacks could operate openly. However, in some states black charitable activities were prohibited by laws enacted in the early nineteenth century. Charitable work had to be done in secret. This was indeed very risky.

African Americans who gained a measure of success always articulated a deep sense of connectedness to their community— not as an erudite philosophical concept but as a personal commitment to give something back. James Forten, the wealthiest black in early nineteenth-century America, began his career as an errand boy in the Philadelphia docks and built his fortune as a sailmaker. Before his death in 1832, he had given away most of his wealth, financially supporting the escape of runaway slaves, purchasing the freedom of others, and contributing to many causes. Nineteenth-century philanthropist Thomy Lafon made substantial contributions to the development of New Orleans. The estate of a black woman in Boston endowed a fund in the 1890s for black students at Harvard Medical School. And Madame C. J. Walker, child of sharecroppers, became a successful and nationally acclaimed businesswoman, the first black millionaire, and a patron of the Harlem Renaissance.

This concept of "giving back" has always differed, I believe, from that of "reciprocity," which is a deeply honored value that has produced historic and often elaborate rituals in many cultures. In reciprocity there is usually the expectation of a mutual or equivalent exchange among persons who know each other or have some kind of relationship. But giving back is an outpouring of gratitude for what has been received (and it may not be a material benefit), often from unknown benefactors. The gift is made to recipients who may also be unknown and there is no expectation of exchange or return. Forten was undoubtedly proud and grateful for the Free African Society's struggles that had paved the way for his success. So he financed the freeing of slaves from whom he could never expect repayment.

Contemporary black philanthropy

Patterns of black giving and volunteering in the twentieth century have been documented by Carson. In "Black Volunteers as Givers and Fundraisers" (paper prepared for the Center for the Study of Philanthropy, City University of New York, 1990), Carson states that in 1989, 60 percent of blacks in households with incomes under $20,000 were givers; 30 percent were both givers and volunteers. In households with incomes over $40,000, 88 percent were givers; 62 percent were both givers and volunteers. Blacks give and volunteer disproportionately to black organizations. Carson observed that traditionally black organizations have relied on their members to be active contributors, volunteers, and fundraisers; this remains the case today.

Blacks have been very generous, and their giving has often been unplanned and spontaneous. Charity is as likely to take the form of spontaneous assistance to persons in need who are taken into one's home or helped in some other way. Although some may criticize spontaneous giving, let us remember that it has been an important way for blacks of all socioeconomic levels to give back—to give through a special collection at church, to respond to an appeal to help a poor bright student get to college, to show solidarity to a community terrorized by a lynching or a cross burning, or to support civil rights movements when even nonviolent challenges to unjust laws were not funded by mainstream foundations.

Spontaneous responses to crises continue to be important. When Spike Lee could not get the additional funding he needed to complete *Malcolm X* and when Henry Hampton required more money for "Eyes on the Prize II," small groups of wealthy blacks responded on short notice and provided the millions of dollars that were needed.

Blacks have not been motivated primarily by the tax advantages of giving. Gifts are often made to organizations like the National Association for the Advancement of Colored People (NAACP), which are not tax-exempt.

Black religious giving

The black church receives more than two-thirds of black charitable dollars. This fact is not attributable merely to the spiritual foundation of black giving. The amount of giving to the black church is a sign of trust in an institution that historically has been controlled by African Americans. I cannot emphasize enough the importance of control to black donors; the question of which entity controls the allocation of charitable dollars is a central one. Giving to the black church also represents an outpouring of thanks for its critical role in establishing other kinds of institutions in areas where public authorities failed to assume their responsibilities.

From the mid-nineteenth century until the 1954 *Brown* v. *Board of Education* decision, black churches collected funds and established educational institutions at all levels—schools, academies, and colleges—in southern and border states. Public facilities were either completely absent or unequal to those provided by the public authorities for white students. Although many, especially the smaller and precollegiate schools, have closed, the black church continues to benefit from a vast reservoir of gratitude for the enormous financial and human investment it made as a leader in educating not only the "talented tenth" but also the masses.

Today, the black church is one of the few institutions that have not abandoned the inner city. It is challenged to address the urban crisis in a contemporary way that gives new life to the spirit and creative risk taking that characterized early black philanthropy in solidarity with the oppressed. It must reenact its role as a spiritual force, a mobilizer of financial and human resources, a builder of institutions that enhance and empower communities during difficult times. Exciting new ventures between foundations and black churches indicate that black churches are strategically positioned to remain vehicles for charitable giving and volunteering. Paternalistic forms of charity that do not engage communities of marginalized people in efforts to solve their own problems will not work. The focus must be on empowerment, capacity building, economic development, and strengthening the infrastructure of inner cities.

Although we tend to focus on Christian churches when we think of black religious institutions, the Muslim community in America is diverse and important. It encompasses immigrants, diplomats, students, employees of multinational corporations who are temporarily assigned here, and African Americans. The American Muslim community is considered one of the most important and rapidly growing in the world of Islam. As Islam has grown over the centuries, indigenous cultures have often shaped the ways in which the faithful fulfill their religious obligations. Charity is one of the five pillars of Islam. Consideration of how American Muslims, and especially African American Muslims, fulfill this religious duty should be included in any discussion about pluralism in philanthropy. We still have so much to learn about all the cultures of giving.

Changing black philanthropy

In recent years, there has been a remarkable increase in the number and variety of vehicles for organized black philanthropy. There are, for instance, the United Negro College Fund (UNCF), charitable programs of Greek-letter and service organizations, and various charitable funds. There are a growing number of black alternative funds. The National Black United Fund, founded in 1972, has fifteen independent fundraising organizations that raised over $7 million in 1990, mostly through payroll deduction plans. During the National Urban League's 1994 annual convention, Hugh Price, the new president, urged each local league to establish a youth development fund, a kind of community foundation that would seek to match a caring adult with every black child. Some of the most innovative black alternative funds combine fundraising, volunteering, and financial commitments by individuals at the local levels. Each of the One Hundred Black Men of Atlanta takes a pledge to make annual contributions to youth programs that seek to enrich educationally, prevent violence, and resolve conflict, and also participates as a mentor and a volunteer.

Establishing a full inventory of independent black charitable funds is difficult. Many are small and not endowed. Some are quite old.

However, we have been surprised at the number that we have been able to locate that are endowed and quite stable. *Donors of Color* (1993), based on a study cosponsored by the Council on Foundations and the Association of Black Foundation Executives, provided a very helpful beginning to understanding the extent of black philanthropy today. But research must continue if we are to understand what motivates blacks today to create charitable funds and what grant-making priorities new funds might have. The Ford Foundation is currently sponsoring diversity projects with twenty community foundations that are expected to produce valuable information and insights about philanthropy in communities of color.

New challenges and opportunities

As the twenty-first century approaches, African American philanthropy confronts new challenges. Although poverty among blacks persists, affluence has risen dramatically. The number of affluent black households increased 360 percent between 1967 and 1987. The income of today's affluent blacks is earned by several workers in the household. Many of these homes are the first in their family history to be rich. They perceive their affluent status to be fragile. Yet they raise the prospect of intergenerational wealth, of black families with substantial inherited wealth over several generations. At the same time, black-owned businesses are growing in number and size and are increasingly operating in the economic mainstream.

Such phenomena raise new questions. What will happen to the cosmology of connectedness and the desire to give back that have characterized the culture of African American giving over the past two centuries? Do the new black millionaires feel connected to the black underclass? Removed at least one generation from the brutal era of enforced segregation and the civil rights movement, will they feel an obligation to a community whose sheltering and sustaining arms they never personally experienced?

Such questions lead to others. What should the message be to nonprofit organizations as they seek new sources of funds in an increasingly competitive environment? What are the prospects for finding large and nontraditional donors in the black community?

Tell them we are rising

The first message is that the culture of giving remains dynamic and vibrant. The strong obligation to give back takes different forms today but remains so central that it is almost taken for granted. Consider the Florida lawyer who gave $10 million a few years ago to the small black college in North Carolina that had admitted him as a poor freshman decades earlier. Consider Dr. Ruth Hayre, a retired school principal who adopted 116 sixth graders at two inner city schools in Philadelphia and promised them full college tuition if they successfully graduated from high school. Hayre's "Tell Them We Are Rising" program takes its name from a moving episode in her own family's history.

As a 10-year-old boy, Hayre's grandfather, born a slave, walked one hundred miles to attend a freedmen's school. When a visiting general asked him for a message to give to the Northerners, the child replied, "Sir, tell them we are rising!" He rose indeed, later founding a black-owned bank in Philadelphia.

The lead story in the *Philadelphia Inquirer*, May 8, 1994, included this comment from Dr. Hayre's account of her decision in 1987 to get involved in philanthropy:

I have explained quite candidly that this is what Reaganomics did for me and for anyone else who had some money to be saved or invested. When Reagan was elected president I knew he would help his wealthy friends. . . . It finally dawned on me that I had more money than I would ever spend and that if I died the next day, a huge amount of it would be taken over as inheritance taxes. The idea of that irked me. As I began to deal with my mortality, I knew I couldn't rest easy in my eventual grave if I had not given of the wealth that had come to me with little exertion. I became almost obsessed with the idea of "giving back." (p. 12)

It is important to note that African Americans who give back do not necessarily limit their gifts to black institutions. With the increased enrollment of blacks in colleges, universities, and professional schools that are white in majority, we can expect to see more black alumni like Reginald F. Lewis whose 1991 gift of $3 million to Harvard Law School was the largest single gift the school had ever received.

More African Americans are searching for ways to give more responsibly. They need more information about tax law provisions, especially regarding options for creating charitable funds. Fundraising in the black community must not be a one-shot drive for the big gift. It must be part of a long-range coordinated effort involving many agencies in the nonprofit world, to educate communities of color about philanthropy and planned giving.

The targets of fundraising should not be just the extraordinarily rich. Outreach efforts should be made to the large number of blacks of moderate means who may not think of themselves as philanthropists but who are the most dependable givers and volunteers. Many could become important donors over time, endowing charitable funds as individuals and families or through multidonor arrangements or organizations to which they belong. They should be approached in their forties and fifties, as they begin to move into their best earning and giving years. They should be encouraged to see philanthropy as a lifetime commitment.

I am convinced that this task must be undertaken at the local level although information could be disseminated at national meetings of black professional associations. America's four hundred community foundations should play a major role in providing leadership for such efforts and in assisting black individuals and organizations to express their charitable impulse in creative and effective ways.

Case studies of successful ventures involving the establishment of charitable funds should be widely shared. The $1 million Christ Fund that was endowed by The Concord Baptist Church of Christ in Brooklyn, New York, for its community service programs, is an excellent model and should be duplicated. Although its mission of "taking the concept of stewardship to another level" is articulated in language that may be traditional, the program is contemporary and relevant.

Increase involvement—and ask!

Acknowledging the close relationship between volunteering and giving, we must recruit more African Americans for membership on important nonprofit boards, both national and local. The black community is largely an untapped source for nontraditional financial support. But prospective black donors to majority-white nonprofits ask tough questions about the racial and ethnic composition of boards and staffs, the constituencies they serve, and the decision makers concerning budgetary allocations. Representative numbers of blacks on the boards are key to developing their trust. But for them to play a vital role in outreach to potential black donors, these individuals must themselves be trusted by the community.

Finally, African Americans must be asked to give! Fundraisers who look to African Americans as a donor community will be surprised by the outcome. In the summer of 1993, fifty-three years after my sister graduated college and at the initiative of a newly hired black development officer, the university she graduated from asked her to endow a scholarship in her name. Within a few weeks, the endowment was established: it will provide one-half of one entering student's freshman tuition for four years. The first scholar enrolled in the fall 1994 term. Why did it take fifty-three years for the request to arrive?

An article in the *Chronicle of Philanthropy* (1994) reported that a group of sixty blacks had raised $536,000 for the San Francisco Public Library's African American Center and plans to raise an additional $500,000. The leader of this effort, Dr. Arthur H. Coleman, reported: "This was the first time the African American community has been brought in at the beginning and asked to play a key role. Usually, by the time the black community hears about a philanthropic project, the train has left the station. If we're lucky, we may catch the caboose. At the library, we are riding first class, and we are paying our way."

Conclusion

Philanthropy in America has been multicultural since the founding of this nation. It is a rich tapestry woven of threads of many different colors and textures. But it is unfinished. Each ethnic group in our generation must weave in more threads and bring diverse and unique cultures of charitable giving into the center of America's philanthropic enterprise.

What should the role of African Americans in philanthropy be today? Philanthropy as connectedness to the brothers and sisters who exist at the margins of our society—the oppressed, the angry, the despairing—has been central to the black experience and to black survival. Surely we have an obligation to bring this message to all philanthropists.

No one has given a more eloquent charge to blacks in philanthropy than Bernard C. Watson before his retirement in 1993 as president of the William Penn Foundation. As the third lecturer in the James A. Joseph Lecture Series, he urged blacks in philanthropy to "make known a different point of view, a different perspective, an angle formed by the prism of their special experience of marginality." Because we ourselves have been outsiders, invisible, our cries to be heard and treated as human beings often ignored, we should "help foundations understand and deal appropriately with the new faces and new voices in American society" (p. 5). We have not been sheltered from the agony of our inner cities, but "we also know something about survival in the face of apparently overwhelming disadvantages and handicaps" (p. 7). We must sensitize foundations to explore the potential for empowerment rather than charity and to take risks with funding small and emerging organizations. But most of all, we must serve as "representatives for the disenfranchised, interpreters for the inarticulate, advocates for the new and potentially risky approaches to grant making" (p. 9).

Who will be the messengers who make, in Watson's words, "a new commitment to bringing to our work our special experience and different perspective"? (p. 10). Black trustees and staff members—whose presence, number, and authority in key areas must be enhanced—are all messengers. The leaders in churches and alternative structures who effectively mobilize dollars and channel them into institutions and community service programs are messengers. African American donors of whatever kind and size, whether they contribute time and treasure to causes and charities or are creators and directors of their own funds, are also messengers.

Wherever we are on this vast philanthropic landscape, we must be faithful to our heritage in order to build on two centuries of connectedness and make it a living reality for our generation and the next generations.

References

Bailey, A. L. "A Library's Appeal: Not by the Book." *Chronicle of Philanthropy*, July 12, 1994, p. 25.

Carson, E. D. "Black Volunteers as Givers and Fundraisers." Paper presented at the Conference on Volunteers and Fundraisers, Center for the Study of Philanthropy, City University of New York, New York, Nov. 14, 1990.

Cudjoe, F. L. "Traditions of African-American Philanthropy in Boston." Paper prepared for the Boston Foundation. Undated.

Joseph, J. A. "Black Philanthropy: The Potential and Limits of Private Generosity in a Civil Society." Paper presented at the first annual Lecture on Black Philanthropy sponsored by the Association of Black Foundation Executives, The Smithsonian Institute, Washington, D.C., June 3, 1991.

Moore, A. "Long-Term Investment." *Philadelphia Inquirer*, May 8, 1994, p. 12.

Watson, B. C. "Minorities and Marginality in American Foundations." Paper presented at the third annual James A. Joseph Lecture sponsored by the Association of Black Foundation Executives, Free Library of Philadelphia, June 11, 1993.

Winters, M. F. *Donors of Color: A Promising New Frontier for Community Foundations.* Washington, D.C.: Council on Foundations and the Association of Black Foundation Executives, 1993.

JEAN E. FAIRFAX *is a consultant to grantmakers on diversity and multiculturalism. She is just completing a three-year project for the Association of Black Foundation Executives called "The Black Presence in Organized Philanthropy."*

*What we don't know about Latino philanthropy can
hurt us. We need more information on Latino traditions of giving, disincentives to Latino philanthropy, and institutional arrangements that might
foster Latino philanthropy. Exploration of these three
issues suggests approaches to Latino philanthropy
that may both improve society and Latino opportunities in society.*

2

Three strategic questions about Latino philanthropy

Michael Cortés

THOSE OF US who study philanthropic behavior do not know as
much as we should about giving by Latinos in the United States.
This ignorance blesses us with a wide and varied universe of potential research topics. But this wealth of unanswered questions are but
empty blessings to date.

Let me begin with what we do know. Latinos—or Hispanics, as
we are called by the federal government—are people of Spanish or
Latin American descent. The United States has the world's fifth
largest Latino population following Mexico, Spain, and the other
Americas. Among Latinos permanently residing in the United
States, eighty percent or fewer are U.S. citizens. Most of the others
are documented immigrants who have obtained permission to live
and work here as permanent residents. By the end of the twentieth

NEW DIRECTIONS FOR PHILANTHROPIC FUNDRAISING, NO. 8, SUMMER 1995 © JOSSEY-BASS PUBLISHERS

century, the Latino minority in the United States will total roughly twenty-five million, approaching 10 percent of the total population. By the year 2010, we will make up the nation's largest minority. High U.S. birthrates and immigration are the causes of the growing numbers of Latinos in the United States (Gann and Duignan, 1986; Mackelprang and Longbrake, 1987.)

When compared with other U.S. residents, Latinos are hardworking, poor, and uneducated. The percentage of them working or seeking work is high. Yet 29 percent live in poverty. Latino workers are concentrated in low-skilled, low-paying jobs. Fewer than 53 percent of Latino adults are high school graduates. Latino youth have the nation's highest high school dropout rates; the typical range in the largest U.S. cities is between 40 and 60 percent. (See Astin, 1982; Borjas and Tienda, 1985; Escutia and Prieto, 1986; Hayes-Bautista, Schink, and Chapa, 1986; National Commission on Secondary Schooling for Hispanics, 1984; Olivas, 1986; Orum, 1986; Santos, 1986; Tienda, 1985; Torres-Gil, 1986; U.S. Congress, 1985; U.S. Department of Commerce 1993, 12–21; U.S. Department of Education, 1980). Research has found that continuing racial and ethnic prejudice limits opportunities for their advancement, exacerbating the social problems already created by low income and education.

However, even this information is misleading. First, it may lead one to believe that Latinos are newcomers to the United States. In fact, Latinos are among our nation's newest immigrants as well as among its oldest families. Indeed, Spanish-speaking people arrived and established communities in Florida and the Southwest long before English speakers arrived. Second, it may lead one to believe that Latinos simply speak Spanish. In fact, the Latino population is made up of Spanish-speaking monolinguals, English-speaking monolinguals, bilinguals, and multilinguals.

Most important of all, the term *Latino* itself is misleading. It is an umbrella term for diverse and distinct subgroups, each with its own problems, characteristics, issues, and philanthropic traditions. Latinos in this nation can be differentiated by ethnic identity, race, and tradition. Of the major backgrounds, 64 percent are of Mexican descent. Nearly 11 percent are Puerto Rican while another 5 percent are Cuban. Almost 14 percent are of Central or South American origin, including substantial populations of Nicaraguans, Salvadorians, and Guatemalans. Latinos come from all the Americas, including the one that calls itself simply *America:* some Latino subcultures originated in regions of the United States and exist only in this country. For example, the Tejanos of south Texas, the 'manitos of New Mexico, and other regional variants of *Chicanismo,* for example, all have distinctive dialects and subcultures found nowhere else.

What we don't know about Latino philanthropy

We know little about Latinos' current patterns of giving. Research findings on Latinos and philanthropy are scant and those we have are discouraging. The research suggests—although not conclusively—that Latinos receive a disproportionately small share of grants from private foundations (Cortés, 1991, pp. 144–146). Research on charitable giving and volunteering conducted by the Gallup Organization for the Independent Sector suggest that Latinos are relatively uncharitable. In those surveys, Virginia Hodgkinson and Murray Weitzman estimate that whereas 72 percent of all U.S. households contribute money to charity, only 53 percent of Latino homes do. Furthermore, those Latinos who do contribute give, on average, smaller percentages of their household income (Hodgkinson and Weitzman, 1992, Table 2.1). The Gallup survey also found that affluent Latinos give only half of what affluent whites and blacks do. For example, among contributing households with more than $40,000 in annual income, African Americans contribute an average of $1,162 per year, whites about $1,251, and Latinos only $594 (Hodgkinson and Weitzman, 1992, Tables 2.4, 2.5, and 2.6).

The Gallup survey has its limitations. First, it relied on self-reporting methods. Second, Hodgkinson and Weitzman's analysis of intergroup differences fails to take differences of wealth (as opposed to income) into account—an important point, as Paul Schervish explains in more detail in another chapter in this book.

Some differences may be explained more by differing religious traditions than by race or ethnicity, as Dean Hoge seems to suggest in the first volume of *Cultures of Giving (New Directions in Philanthropic Fundraising*, no. 7). Finally, Latino traditions include other forms of philanthropy besides money and labor donated to nonprofit organizations. Perhaps those forms of giving are more important among Latinos than among other groups. If so, the survey would have a built-in bias against Latinos.

A study done by Bradford Smith and his associates at the University of San Francisco (1994) suggests that the definition used for the Gallup–Independent Sector survey is too culture bound, so that the survey underestimates giving by ethnic minorities. Smith's project explored patterns of philanthropy for African American, Mexican, Guatemalan, Salvadorian, Filipino, Chinese, Japanese, and Korean groups living in the San Francisco Bay Area. He found their philanthropic traditions and their forms and patterns of giving so qualitatively different even from one another that he advised against attempting the sort of quantitative intergroup comparisons made by the Gallup survey.

Smith views philanthropy as a form of social exchange benefiting both those who give and those who receive rather than as a one-way transaction. But we must be careful even here. Smith's broader view of ethnic philanthropy poses a conceptual problem. Broadly inclusive definitions of philanthropy risk making it nearly indistinguishable from economic transactions and other social exchanges. The definition of giving used by Hodgkinson and Weitzman is problematical, as Smith and his colleagues demonstrate. But although helpful, Smith's approach may lack precision. The very concept of philanthropy, like the concept of the Latino minority, can limit our understanding of Latino philanthropy.

It is clear that Latino philanthropy varies among subgroups and is qualitatively distinctive. But quantitatively speaking, the net value given per person is hard to measure in any meaningful way. In short, apart from differences that come from household wealth, income, and population size, researchers do not know whether the sum of

Latino philanthropy, in all its forms, is measurably different from other U.S. populations.

Three strategic questions

The data raise several ethical question for all fundraisers. Should non-Latino charities ask Latinos for support even if most of them neglect Latino interests? The data also pose a question specifically for Latinos. If non-Latino philanthropy discriminates against us, what should we do about it? What are we prepared to do for ourselves? How can we improve our own prospects, promote justice, and contribute to society and humanity as a whole? How will our own ethnic, regional, linguistic, and historical divisions complicate the future development of Latino philanthropy? These questions are all important. But they are difficult to answer.

What we don't know about Latino philanthropy can hurt us. There are missed opportunities to develop Latino philanthropy in ways that improve society and the place and opportunities for Latinos within society. Indeed, the hope of benefiting Latinos and the rest of society by cultivating, expanding, and redirecting Latino philanthropy is reason enough to learn more.

Research on Latino philanthropy should focus on three strategic questions: (1) Which community traditions might predispose Latinos to give more? (2) Does society provide disincentives that discourage Latino philanthropy? (3) What new organizational and institutional arrangements might foster and facilitate Latino philanthropy?

Although hard data about Latino philanthropy are lacking, there are many opinions on the subject. Veterans of community self-help and empowerment movements are a rich source of ideas and anecdotes on the subject. I cannot claim to be able to document all their opinions (although Estrada, 1990, provides a model for doing so). I cannot even clearly distinguish between my opinions and those of others. In addition, my views are colored by my primary exposure

to Chicano communities in the Southwest and my relative ignorance of other Latino traditions. Nevertheless, in this chapter I offer
what I consider to be valuable hunches about the answers future
research may provide to these three strategic questions.

Which community traditions might predispose Latinos to give more?

Despite their cultural heterogeneity, Latinos share three strong philanthropic traditions: they rely on extended family networks to help
those in need; they donate time and money to the Catholic Church;
and they create *mutualistas*, or mutual assistance associations, to
enable community survival in politically, socially, and economically
hostile environments. Camarillo (1991) describes Chicano mutualistas in the Southwest. Rodríguez-Fraticelli, Sanabria, and Tirado
(1991) provide a comparable history of Puertorriqueño mutual assistance organizations in New York.

When it extends beyond family and church, Latino philanthropy
is mediated by personal exchange relationships based on trust. Over-
lying the three common traditions, then, is that of *personalismo*, an
emphasis on the personal relationship. Trust is the cumulative product of personal relationships based on mutual assistance and exchange. Latinos are like other ethnic groups in this respect. But
fundraisers should not assume that their institution's mission and reputation is enough to gain the trust of Latinos. Latinos often seek a
personal guarantee from an individual they trust that their donations
will indeed be used in ways they value. Many Latinos value programs
benefiting members of their own communities in particular.

The three traditions of philanthropy, and especially the third one
of mutual assistance, provide a cultural foundation on which strategies to foster philanthropy might be built. Throughout most of this
century, labor union and community organizers have tried to promote self-help and cooperation by defending and renewing the
community identities of Latinos and creating a greater sense of solidarity among them. That strategy is partly responsible for the
growing number of Latino nonprofit organizations in the United

States (see Estrada, 1991). Fundraisers for non-Latino nonprofits might consider developing joint campaigns with these Latino organizations, in which benefits to Latino communities would be obvious to potential donors.

Hard-won economic and political participation in the larger society is the result in part of increased community organizing and activism over the past few decades. This activism built on the tradition of *mutualistas*, which were formed in the nineteenth and early twentieth centuries that contributed to the Latino community empowerment movements in the 1950s, 1960s, and 1970s. More recently, Latino immigrants have also sustained themselves with the traditions of mutual assistance they brought with them from other countries (Smith, Shue, Vest, and Villarreal, 1994, Chapters 3–5). But with Latinos' increased mobility and partial success at economic, political, and social integration, the traditions of mutual assistance must either adapt or perish. Indeed, assimilation into mainstream society, while beneficial in many respects, has also put at risk some Latino values and traditions, which are being stretched thin by geographic mobility and assaulted by the demands and expectations of powerful non-Latino social institutions.

In the case of traditional philanthropy, there may be more erosion than evolution. Urban labor markets, medical insurance, zoning laws, schools, and popular culture—all promote individualism and the nuclear family, not the extended family. Geographic mobility and exposure to Protestantism are eroding Latinos' traditional ties to Catholic parishes. Many of the original *mutualistas* have already disappeared (Camarillo, 1991).

Despite its technical limitations and narrow definition of philanthropical activity, the Gallup survey has, I suspect, revealed a disturbing truth: upwardly mobile Latinos (even though their mobility may be limited when compared with other U.S. populations) and even more so the children of these individuals tend to disengage themselves from traditional forms of philanthropy. Incomplete integration and acceptance of affluent Latinos by the rest of U.S. society might foster more anomie than philanthropy.

If my hunches about Latino community traditions are correct, there are lessons for fundraisers. Obviously, they must learn about and build upon Latinos' traditions of mutual assistance and trust in personal relationships in all their local variations. "Latinos helping Latinos" would be a productive theme for fundraising strategies and campaigns, for example. Recent political organizing in Chicago illustrates how diverse ethnic subgroups can join together with a single Latino identity. But more typical are Miami and other cities where ethnically diverse Latino populations usually call themselves Cubans, Nicaraguans, and so on. Thus, Guatemalans helping Guatemalans, Puerto Ricans helping Puerto Ricans, Tejanos del Valle del Rio Grande helping their own, and so forth, might be even more effective fundraising themes. So, too, would campaigns among immigrants that promise help to victims of misfortune in their homelands.

Of course, ethical fundraisers would have to assume personal responsibility for assuring that the donations are used in the ways promised. Mere tokenism about Latino community benefits would soon prove counterproductive. Abuse of trust would accelerate erosion of remaining traditional foundations for Latino philanthropy.

Another Independent Sector analysis found that the nonprofit sector has lagged behind the public and for-profit sectors in hiring Latinos: 5.3 percent, compared to 6.4 percent in government and 8.6 percent in the for-profit sector (Hispanics in Philanthropy, 1994, p. 3). To raise more funds from Latinos, fundraisers should help clients integrate Latinos into nonprofit boards and staff. If my speculation proves right, Latino donations of money and volunteer labor will go to those nonprofits that succeed in increasing Latino involvement in defining—and benefiting from—the organization's mission and priorities.

Fundraisers understandably focus their individual fundraising efforts on potentially large donors. Soliciting smaller donors is often relegated to direct mail efforts and to federated fundraising campaigns. Yet anecdotal evidence suggests that direct mail campaigns have not enjoyed much success with Latinos. Perhaps mailing lists have not been compiled with the distinctive demographics of Latinos in mind. Perhaps the expertise of nonprofit direct mail organizations lags behind that of firms in the for-profit sector, where there is greater appreciation and understanding of the nation's growing Latino markets. (For more on marketing to Latinos, see Guernica and Kasperuk, 1982; Kotkin, 1987; Valencia, 1989.)

In contrast to direct mail's relative lack of success in fundraising, televised appeals to help innocent victims of disasters seem to be remarkably effective. An impromptu appeal on Spanish language television for aid after the recent earthquake in Mexico City reportedly produced hundreds of thousands of dollars from U.S. audiences with unprecedented speed.

Does society provide special disincentives that discourage Latino philanthropy?

Latinos have fewer opportunities for low-cost giving to nonprofit organizations than do other groups. This is because cost of giving always includes not only the amount donated but also hidden costs. Federated fundraising campaigns offer significant opportunities for low-cost giving. But research on the United Way and other federated campaigns may show that they have served non-Latinos better than Latinos.

To understand why, it helps once again to think of philanthropy as a social exchange. Both parties to the exchange experience costs and benefits. The benefits to donors may be intangible, but are certainly gratifying. But donors must spend time considering how best to allocate their gifts in order to increase their satisfaction in giving. Donors take risks when they decide to give money to people who might not live up to their promises. Risk is a hidden cost of giving.

Fundraising campaigns like the United Way, the Combined Federal Campaign, and other funds such as the National Service Agencies and the Black United Crusades, reduce the hidden costs of charitable giving for both donors and recipients. Donors can make a single pledge decision based on the reputation and stability of a local branch of the organization. Payment by payroll deduction removes even further the time and anxiety costs of making an annual pledge.

Local United Way agencies have long been criticized for failing to fund Latino nonprofits serving Latino communities. (See, for example, Castillo, 1988, p. 103; Cruz, 1988; and National Committee for Responsive Philanthropy, 1989, p. 3, and 1990, p. 1.) Getting them to include Latino community interests has been a frustratingly slow process. Giving to an unresponsive United Way agency clearly runs counter to Latino traditions of *mutualista* in hostile environments. Thus, the United Way enjoys little trust within Latino communities and at the same time Latino giving through alternative channels is discouraged by higher hidden costs.

The designated beneficiary option offered by some United Way campaigns could reduce Latinos' mistrust of the organization, especially if the option were marketed effectively by trustworthy individuals known to Latinos. Another alternative is to stimulate giving to organizations other than the United Way altogether.

At the time she did her master's thesis, Lilia Frankel Castillo found that selected Latino community leaders in the Los Angeles area had more hope of reforming United Way, in spite of their anger and resentment toward that agency, than they did of starting an alternative fundraising federation (Castillo, 1988, pp. 77–90). At the time, African American alternative federated fundraising drives were making inroads among Latinos. Significant numbers of Latinos in the Los Angeles area gave in response to telephone solicitations by the Brotherhood Crusade, organized by African American community activists. The Brotherhood Crusade, in return, allocated funds to local Latino community service agencies. More recently, however, the United Latino Fund was launched in Los Angeles with significant foundation and corporate donations and operating subsidies. The fund is working with the Los Angeles County Chicano Employees Association, among others, to develop an individual donor pool and payroll deduction program. Other alternative funds, such as the Hispanic Federation in New York City, were even formed with support from local United Way organizations.

Most Latino nonprofits are of little help when it comes to promoting Latino philanthropy, often bypassing potential Latino donors. Most find that fundraising among individuals is less cost-effective than seeking grants or contracts from government agencies, businesses, or foundations. Yet fundraisers for Latino nonprofits are better positioned than other organizations to succeed at direct mail and donor acquisition campaigns in Latino communities. Their staffs are more sensitive to local traditions and norms; their programs allow more honest, consistent appeals to Latino community traditions of mutual assistance. To their disadvantage, however, Latino nonprofits usually lack the sophistication and resources needed to develop an effective campaign. I rarely hear of Latino nonprofits hiring experienced, well-qualified fundraisers for their staffs or as consultants.

What new organizational and institutional arrangements might foster and facilitate Latino philanthropy?

Should affluent and wealthy Latinos be encouraged to give to community foundations? Are private family foundations likely to suit wealthy Latinos? What other kinds of organizational models appear promising? How might the "philanthropic climates" described by Teresa Odendahl be modified to encourage Latino philanthropy (Odendahl, 1987, pp. 234–236)?

Some community foundations, such as those in El Paso, Texas, and Miami, are trying outreach programs to attract previously uninvolved Latino donors. Some United Way agencies, as mentioned earlier, are experimenting with sponsorship of Latino alternative funds. Conventionally incorporated Latino philanthropies in the United States are new and few in number. It is not clear yet what their long-term missions and strategies will be nor what models they will develop or adopt.

The United Latino Fund in Los Angeles receives large grants and distributes the funds to Latino nonprofits submitting competitive proposals. The fund is also developing a base of individual small donors. But it is inventing its own program as it goes. It remains to be seen whether it will seek, or even accept, endowments or whether its organizers will create another organization for that purpose.

Groups in other cities have tried other approaches. The Greater Kansas City Hispanic Development Fund, established by the Hall Family Foundation with support from other private and corporate foundations, has functioned primarily as a pass-through organization involving board members and local Latino advisors. In San Francisco, the Hispanic Community Fund of the Bay Area began as a joint project of the Bay Area United Way and the National Concilio of America. Hispanics in Philanthropy, a professional association of trustees and staff of private foundations and corporate contributions programs, organizes fora at which its members develop models of organized philanthropy together with emerging philanthropies based in Latin America.

Latino nonprofits may be able to initiate organizational and institutional arrangements for fostering and facilitating Latino philanthropy. Here are some ideas to explore, perhaps through demonstration projects involving concerned foundations and Latino nonprofits with community organizing expertise.

First, Latino nonprofits could target wealthy Latino entrepreneurs to encourage them to adopt the corporate contribution practices used by other successful companies. Whatever their personal cultural background, wealthy Latinos in the United States are likely to have acquired, or at least maintained, their wealth by adapting to the norms of the competitive domestic market and corporate philanthropy is an increasingly accepted practice in the business circles in which affluent Latinos function. The nation's leading Latino businesses are a good place to begin such efforts. *Hispanic Business* magazine, starting with the 1984 issue (Balkan, 1984a, b), offers a listing of these businesses that is updated annually.

Latino business and professional associations are another potential target. These associations include the National Hispanic Bar Association, the Hispanic Business and Women's Professional Association, the Hispanic Corporate Council, Hispanics in Philanthropy, the Latin American Manufacturers Association, the Personnel Management Association of Aztlán, the Society of Hispanic Professional Engineers, and the U.S. Hispanic Chamber of Commerce. Local Hispanic chambers of commerce and other associations could also be contacted. The Los Angeles area alone is home to the Latin Business Association, the Mexican-American Bar Association, and the Mexican American Grocers Association. Publications targeted to the Hispanic community, such as *Hispanic Business* and *Hispanic Entrepreneur*, might also promote models of philanthropy. Expanded Latino corporate philanthropy might then be a precursor to more personal forms of giving later on.

Several leading Latino nonprofit organizations could collaborate in developing and implementing these strategies. The National Council of La Raza, for example, has provided training, management, and technical assistance to Latino community-based organizations for decades. The council expanded and diversified its corporate support when the Reagan administration eliminated the remaining vestiges of the War on Poverty and Great Society programs on which the council and other Latino nonprofits had depended. The experience of these organizations could be helpful in developing and legitimating models of corporate philanthropy among Latino business people.

Latino nonprofits could also promote Latino philanthropy by seeking more donations from wealthy and affluent Latinos. This approach could be a precursor to other forms of Latino philanthropy, such as donating to community foundations and starting private grant making foundations.

There are still other ways for Latino nonprofits with community organizing experience to stimulate Latino philanthropy. Castillo (1988, pp. 90–100) explores past and future prospects for developing community-based fundraising and philanthropy in the Los Angeles Latino community. The Community Services Organization, for instance, funds a wide variety of services to the Latino community through a combination of fees from various programs, grass-roots fundraising, and diverse program grants and contracts from public agencies and private foundations. In this way, a respected nonprofit and Latino community leaders can help define new community norms for individual charitable giving.

Organized labor might also be a resource for increasing charitable giving. Union locals with high proportions of Latino membership might adopt and help promote charitable activities and norms. Appropriate models might be explored with the AFL-CIO Labor Council for Latin American Advancement. Major Latino employers might also take the lead in promoting employee community involvement and social responsibility programs, by adapting community service models pioneered by firms like Levi Strauss & Co. Employee contribution programs, no matter how small, strengthen philanthropic norms among employers. Even token contributions by employees of Latino firms should promote more exemplary philanthropic behavior by employers.

Indeed, innovative fundraising programs by Latino nonprofits might lead to new models for promoting Latino charitable contributions in general, for more ambitious forms of personal philanthropy. The Mexican American Legal Defense and Educational Fund (MALDEF), for example, is building upon Latinos' traditional mutual assistance norms by reaching out to selected affluent Latinos. MALDEF has raised funds from Latinos standing to benefit from various class-action civil rights suits brought by the organization. In the late 1980s, of the ninety-five contributors of funds for MALDEF's suit against Los Angeles County on voting redistricting, the large majority were affluent Latino individuals, businessmen, or public officials residing within the voting districts in question. During the same period, MALDEF raised funds from Latino employees of the U.S. Customs Service when it was also suing the Customs Service for discriminating against Latino employees. MALDEF's new approach to fundraising is but a small part of the organization's overall fundraising program. However, although successful at individual fundraising (when compared with other Latino nonprofits), MALDEF continues to depend on foundation grants and corporate contributions for the bulk of its income (MALDEF, 1988, p. 18).

Conclusion

We do not know as much as we should about Latino philanthropy. What we do know is worrisome, as has been developed above. Nor do we know which strategies to use to increase Latino philanthropy.

Our ignorance about Latino philanthropy is an important problem. In this chapter, I have maintained that future research should focus on three questions for informing future strategies. Given today's dearth of information on the subject, we can only speculate about the best strategies to employ. Answers to the questions I pose, which I hope will be provided by future research, will put us on firmer ground in developing strategies for increasing Latino philanthropy in ways Latinos find meaningful and worthwhile.

At this moment, we can only speculate about how best to increase Latino philanthropy. I believe three questions in particular can help guide researchers: What community traditions might predispose Latinos to give more? Do the incidental, hidden costs of giving, such as information and transaction costs and risk, pose a relatively large disincentive for Latino philanthropy? What new organizational and institutional arrangements would facilitate more giving? I have suggested some possibilities above.

The Latino culture of giving is diverse, divided by many factors including both demographic and national factors. But there are also common characteristics and traditions. The integrity of Latino communities and social forces encouraging assimilation are constantly in tension. What we don't know offers us an opportunity to ask useful questions. We should not waste scarce resources for research on Latino philanthropy by funding studies that belabor the question of whether Latinos are more or less charitable than other U.S. populations? Rather, we should focus on identifying and testing strategies for increasing Latino philanthropy.

References

Astin, A. W. *Final Report of the Commission on the Higher Education of Minorities.* Los Angeles: Higher Education Research Institute, 1982.

Balkan, D. C. "The Hispanic Business 400 in Sales." (Annual update.) *Hispanic Business,* June 1984a, pp. 24–42.

Balkan, D. C. "100 Influentials." *Hispanic Business,* May 1984b, pp. 18–27.

Borjas, G. J., and Tienda, M. (eds.). *Hispanics in the U.S. Economy.* New York: Academic Press, 1985.

Camarillo, A. "Mexican Americans and Nonprofit Organizations: An Historical Overview." In H. E. Gallegos and M. O'Neill (eds.), *Hispanics and the Nonprofit Sector.* New York: Foundation Center, 1991.

Castillo, L. F. "An Exploratory-Descriptive Study of the Historical Development of Independent Fundraising in the Los Angeles Chicano Community." M.S.W. thesis, University of California, Los Angeles, 1988.

Cortés, M. "Philanthropy and Latino Nonprofits: A Research Agenda." In H. E. Gallegos and M. O'Neill (eds.), *Hispanics and the Nonprofit Sector.* New York: Foundation Center, 1991.

Cruz, J. *United Way Support to Puerto Rican Organizations: An Assessment.* Washington, D.C.: National Puerto Rican Coalition, 1988.

Escutia, M. M., and Prieto, M. *Hispanics in the Work Force.* Washington, D.C.: National Council of la Raza, 1986.

Estrada, L. F. "Hispanic Evolution: As Their Giving Evolves, Many Hispanics Link Philanthropy to Personal Involvement in Civic Affairs." *Foundation News,* May/June 1990, pp. 34–36.

Estrada, L. F. "Survival Profiles on Latino Nonprofit Organizations." In H. E. Gallegos and M. O'Neill (eds.), *Hispanics and the Nonprofit Sector.* New York: Foundation Center, 1991.

Gann, L. H., and Duignan, P.J. *The Hispanics in the United States.* Boulder, Colo.: Westview Press, 1986.

Guernica, A., and Kasperuk, I. *Reaching the Hispanic Market Effectively: The Media, the Market, the Methods.* New York: McGraw-Hill, 1982.

Hayes-Bautista, D. E., Schink, W. O., and Chapa, J. *The Burden of Support: The Young Latino Population in an Aging American Society.* Stanford, Calif.: Stanford University Press, 1986.

Hispanics in Philanthropy. "Latinos Represent 5.3 Percent of Nonprofit Sector." *Hispanics in Philanthropy News,* Summer 1994, p. 3.

Hodgkinson, V. A., and Weitzman, M. A. *Giving and Volunteering in the United States: Findings from a National Survey.* Washington, D.C.: Independent Sector, 1992.

Kotkin, J. "Selling to the New America." *Inc.* July 1987, pp. 44–47.

Mackelprang, A. J., and Longbrake, D. B. "Hispanic Population Growth and Economic Development: Setting the Policy Agenda for the Next Century." *Management Science and Policy Analysis,* 1987, *4* (4), 19–29.

Mexican American Legal Defense and Educational Fund (MALDEF). *Annual Report: May 1987 to April 1988.* Los Angeles, 1988.

National Commission on Secondary Schooling for Hispanics. *Make Something*

Happen. Commission Report. Washington, D.C.: Hispanic Policy Development Project, 1984.

National Committee for Responsive Philanthropy. *Responsive Philanthropy.* (Newsletter) Washington, D.C.: National Committee for Responsive Philanthropy, Winter 1989.

National Committee for Responsive Philanthropy. *Responsive Philanthropy.* (Newsletter) Washington, D.C.: National Committee for Responsive Philanthropy, Spring 1990.

Odendahl, T. "Wealthy Donors and Their Charitable Attitudes." In T. Odendahl (ed.), *America's Wealthy and the Future of Foundations.* New York: Foundation Center, 1987.

Olivas, M. (ed.). *Latino College Students.* New York: Teachers College Press, 1986.

Orum, L. S. *The Education of Hispanics: Status and Implications.* Washington, D.C.: National Council of la Raza, 1986.

Rodríguez-Fraticelli, C., Sanabria, C., and Tirado, A. "Puerto Rican Nonprofit Organizations in New York City." In H. E. Gallegos and M. O'Neill (eds.), *Hispanics and the Nonprofit Sector.* New York: Foundation Center, 1991.

Santos, R. *Hispanic Youth: Emerging Workers.* New York: Praeger, 1986.

Smith, B., Shue, S., Vest, J. L., and Villarreal, J. *Ethnic Philanthropy: Sharing and Giving Money, Goods, and Services in the African American, Mexican, Chinese, Japanese, Filipino, Korean, Guatemalan, and Salvadoran Communities of the San Francisco Bay Area.* San Francisco: Institute for Nonprofit Organization Management, College of Professional Studies, University of San Francisco, 1994.

Tienda, M. "The Puerto Rican Worker: Current Labor Market Status and Future Prospects." *Journal of Hispanic Politics,* 1985, *1* (1), 27–51.

Torres-Gil, F. (ed.). "Hispanics in an Aging Society." New York: Carnegie Corporation of New York, 1986.

U.S. Congress. Congressional Research Service. "Hispanic Children in Poverty." No. 85–170-EPW. Washington, D.C., 1985.

U.S. Department of Commerce. Bureau of the Census. *1980 Census of Population. Vol. 1.: Characteristics of the Population. Ch. 1: Detailed Population Characteristics. Part 1: United States Summary. Sec. A: United States.* Washington, D.C.: U.S. Government Printing Office, 1981.

U.S. Department of Commerce. Bureau of the Census. "The Hispanic Population in the United States, March 1992." *Current Population Reports, Population Characteristics,* P20–465RV. Washington, D.C.: U.S. Government Printing Office, 1993.

U.S. Department of Education. National Center for Education Statistics. *The Condition of Education for Hispanic Americans.* Washington, D.C., 1980.

Valencia, H. "Growth at the High End." *Hispanic Business,* May 1989, pp. 28–32.

MICHAEL CORTÉS *is assistant professor of public policy at the University of Colorado at Denver, School of Public Affairs. His publications include "Philanthropy and Latinos: A Research Agenda."*

World events and demographic trends among Amer-
ican Jews suggest changes in giving patterns and
some structural problems for Jewish philanthropy. A
renewed focus on Jewish identity will be a prerequi-
site to continued raising of funds for Jewish causes.

3

New directions in contemporary Jewish philanthropy: The challenges of the 1990s

Barry A. Kosmin

THIS CHAPTER suggests that cultures of giving are not fixed. Rather, they change and develop in response to world events and social trends. The specific thesis developed here is that organized American Jewish philanthropy faces a new situation now that the political and societal goals that made up the communal agenda for most of this century have been achieved. These positive but unexpected events have made necessary a thorough rethinking of the culture of giving. The paradox in this success is that the main thrust of American Jewish philanthropy is now challenged. By the 1980s an important historic change had already occurred: a majority of philanthropic dollars from American Jews were going to support general rather than specifically Jewish charities (Kosmin and Ritterband, 1991). Thus a reassessment of the goals, focus, methods, and constituency for Jewish fundraising is required. The reduction in external threats, at home and abroad, requires a new emphasis on inner-directed rather than

NEW DIRECTIONS FOR PHILANTHROPIC FUNDRAISING, NO. 8, SUMMER 1995 © JOSSEY-BASS PUBLISHERS

outer-directed goals. However, for this to occur a new generation needs to be socialized and motivated for involvement in the Jewish philanthropic endeavor.

Historical changes

American Jewish philanthropy in the twentieth century, and particularly since 1945 following the tragic occurrence of the Holocaust in Nazi Germany, has been largely devoted to rescuing endangered and oppressed Jewish communities around the world and to securing a viable Jewish homeland in Israel. But in recent years, work toward these goals has met with unprecedented and unexpected success. And like all change, success has its price. The "New World Order" is likely to change dramatically the traditional pattern of Jewish philanthropic endeavor because American Jews have historically used donation to Israel and other overseas causes as an expression of their attitudes about both Israel and their own Jewish identities.

The demise of the Soviet Union removes the emphasis on Jewish communities in danger and the crisis mode of fundraising. The political campaigns to free Soviet, Ethiopian, and Syrian Jews were successful and have resulted in large-scale migration to Israel. It is likely that the Operation Exodus campaign launched in 1990—a three-year campaign to raise $420 million for the 200,000 immigrants expected during that period—was the last of its type. New donors were swept up by the excitement. The target was raised to $1 billion. Donors were pressured to advance their payments after 185,000 immigrants arrived in Israel in 1990. In four years the campaign ended short of its goal but with a respectable $910 million raised. Whether the individual Exodus Campaign hurt annual campaigns—creating a sort of donor and solicitor burnout—or assisted it by attracting new donors to the United Jewish Appeal (UJA)/Federation system is still being debated, but in any case a similar effort is unlikely to be repeated soon.

The state of Israel has seen the fulfillment of the Zionist dream beyond the dreams even of its founders. On the philosophical level, it has been particularly successful in the area of *kibbutz galuyot*, the prophecized gathering of exiles from Asia, Africa, and Europe. On the secular level, it has emerged as a politically stable democracy with a strong military and economic presence. Diplomatic and economic isolation has ended. In 1994 Israel is a modern, technologically sophisticated society, with a population exceeded in number of engineers per capita only by Japan. As a result it has moved in a few decades from a third world to a Western standard of living. In the last five years, after initial problems associated with the integration of the sudden influx of over five hundred thousand refugees, the society has become more self-sufficient and self-assured. Both of these related developments—the removal of the Soviet threat with its accompanying support of Arab intransigence and the mass migration to Israel—have in turn encouraged the Middle East peace process.

Gary Tobin (1994) concluded from his recent research among philanthropic donors that "the redefinition of a positive new relationship between Diaspora Jews and Israel beyond the narrow confines of the crisis campaign must be the central concern of the future." American Jews have sent about $1.5 billion annually to Israel over the last decade. But the gross domestic product (GDP) of Israel has soared to $65 billion today from $20 billion in the 1980s. Motivated by a desire to change the terms of the their traditional relationship—their dependent position as a poor relation— a new generation of Israeli politicians led by the Labor Party's Deputy Foreign Minister Yossi Beilin has begun to question the fundamental structure and purpose of American Jewry's philanthropic operation. The recognition that a new era has indeed emerged was symbolized in June 1994 by a conference on Israel-Diaspora relations in Jerusalem convened and chaired by President Ezer Weitzman that brought American Jewry's philanthropic leadership together with Israel's intellectual and political elite to discuss a new form of partnership.

Demographic trends

These developments on the world scene have been matched by internal changes among American Jews. Both individually and collectively American Jews are more accepted in U.S. society today than ever before. General levels of anti-Semitism have diminished. Exclusionary practices in the economic sphere, restrictive regulations in housing, and quotas in Ivy League colleges, all in force in the 1950s, have now vanished. At the same time, extended families and concentrated ethnic neighborhoods have also largely vanished. Rates of residential mobility are high. Traditional forms of Judaism have lost adherents and the general level of religious practice and behavior has declined. And since "people give to people," as it is said, these trends have been detrimental to the social networks that promote both community involvement and philanthropy.

The findings of the Council of Jewish Federations' 1990 National Jewish Population Survey show profound effects on the self-image of the U.S. Jewish community (Kosmin and others, 1991). The findings confirmed that American Jewry has achieved socioeconomic success and social integration. The study found a more "American" and less "Jewish" population, a geographically mobile and increasingly unaffiliated and secularized population. This idea was symbolized by the much-heralded finding that 52 percent of marriages involving a Jew in the 1985–90 period were interfaith unions. The consequences of interfaith marriage on Jewish philanthropy are clear. Although the propensity to donate to secular charities does not vary between endogamous and exogamous couples, the likelihood of giving to a Jewish charity declines from 62 percent to 28 percent of households.

The demographic picture that emerged from the 1990 survey also suggested some medium-term structural problems for communal philanthropy. Half of adult American Jews are "baby boomers" (see Figure 3.1). In addition, the baby boomers are now producing a "baby boomlet." At the same time, compared with the total U.S. population there is an overrepresentation of the elderly, and particularly those over 75 years. Finally, there is a "missing generation"—

Figure 3.1. The Missing Generation: Age Structure of Jewish Population, in Five-Year Increments

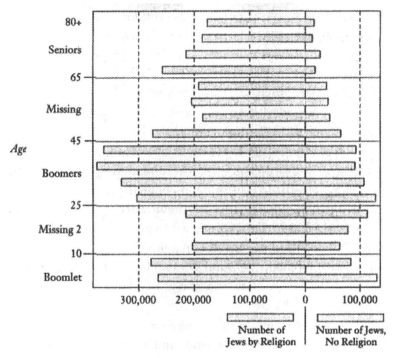

Source: Council of Jewish Federations

the so-called empty nesters aged 50 to 64—as a result of low Jewish birthrates during the Depression and World War II. There are two thirty-something Jews for every fifty-something Jew. People in this age group, usually at the height of their earning power, traditionally have formed the foundation for both volunteer and leadership groups. But this group is currently thin. As a result of these demographic realities, in terms of the philanthropic economy of a volunteer community, dependency ratios are quite high.

The social outlook and Jewish identity of the baby boomers is also a challenge to past patterns of organized *tzedakah*, Jewish philanthropy, and *maasim tovim*, good deeds or voluntarism. Achievements were based on efficient fundraising techniques geared toward a wealthy and generous donor elite who were imbued with a spirit of noblesse oblige, itself sustained by high levels of emotional solidarity with recipients. The traditional cultural and religious attachments that validated and informed this process through reminders of biblical injunctions, such as the command to "ransom captives" or Maimonides' medieval dictum that the highest form of charity involves anonymous donors and recipients, have changed. Communitarian impulses have been replaced by consumerism and an emphasis on the individual. The baby boom generation is less attracted to the umbrella concept of the community chest—the annual United Jewish Appeal/Federation campaign. A preference for designated giving is growing in popularity instead. As a result, in real (inflation-adjusted) dollars, the annual campaign that eroded between 1970 and 1980 continued to erode between 1980 and 1990. It should be noted that the amounts collected are still impressive—$805 million in 1992 and $793 million in 1993. Increasingly, however, the campaign is "top heavy" (see Figure 3.2) in terms of gifts and age of the givers.

Socioeconomic and occupational change is also affecting the American Jewish culture of giving. American Jews are a very educated population. As a result, their overall occupational profile is now dominated by the professional and managerial classes rather than the formerly dominant commercial and entrepreneurial classes. This means that the traditional UJA style of solicitation and campaigning through group expectation and pressure at dinners is increasingly ineffective. This is particularly so because American Jews are the most egalitarian population group in U.S. society. Jewish women are three times more likely than other white women to graduate from college and four times more likely to complete postgraduate degrees. This means that a high proportion of Jewish households contain dual-career "yuppie" couples. Yet little attention has been devoted to investigating the dynamics of giving among egalitarian baby boomer couples.

Women's roles and issues are now a crucial consideration for Jewish philanthropy both in terms of fundraising and of voluntarism.

Figure 3.2. Total Gifts and Dollars Contributed by Campaign (1993 Totals for All North American Federations)

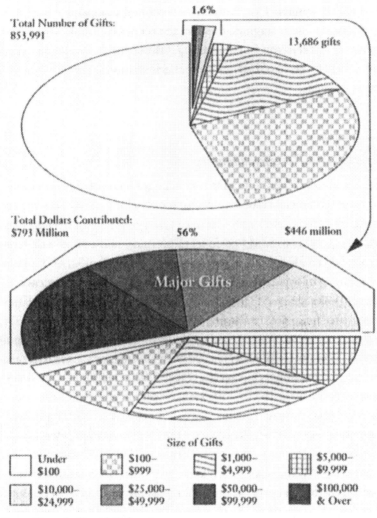

Total Number of Gifts: 853,991

1.6%

13,686 gifts

Total Dollars Contributed: $793 Million

56%

$446 million

Major Gifts

Size of Gifts

Under $100 $100–$999 $1,000–$4,999 $5,000–$9,999

$10,000–$24,999 $25,000–$49,999 $50,000–$99,999 $100,000 & Over

Source: Council of Jewish Federations

The emerging generation of young career women finds the traditional "old boys' club" and its practices alienating (Kosmin, 1989). Thus, the ideological and practical role of federation women's divisions is a challenge. Contributions to women's campaigns rose while overall campaigns stagnated during the recent economic downturn. In an era of "relationship marketing," the separate campaign makes sense. But in terms of integration and institutional power it has its disadvantages.

Investing in Jewish identity

The institutional solution to these challenges has been a new emphasis on total financial resource development, a long-range strategy to finance the federation system from a variety of funding streams. The primary goal is to build up federation endowment programs (see Figure 3.3) and secure in perpetuity some of the wealth of the older generation of loyal givers by means of bequests. Great success has already been achieved. Total federation endowment and foundation assets rose from $600 million in 1981 to nearly $2.7 billion in 1991. Permanent endowment assets tripled to $1 billion during the same period. The potential is certainly there among the more than one million Jewish seniors alive today. Over 55,000 elderly Jews die every year, but according to the National Jewish Population Survey, less than 10 percent leave bequests to Jewish charities. UJA/Federation organizations currently receive less than a thousand bequests each year. As a result, a new initiative, Perpetual Annual Campaign Endowment (PACE), was undertaken in 1993 to solicit endowments specifically for the perpetuation of annual campaign gifts from loyal donors who are wedded to this form of philanthropy. Some federations presently receive more than 20 percent of their annual campaign revenue from the proceeds of philanthropic funds and supporting foundations, although the national average is approximately 10 percent. The encouragement of Jewish federation-controlled charitable trusts is now also an important strategy both locally and nationally.

**Figure 3.3. Federation Capital Base Format:
The Changing Relationship Between Annual Campaign
Allocations and Endowment Foundation Assets, 1976–1993**

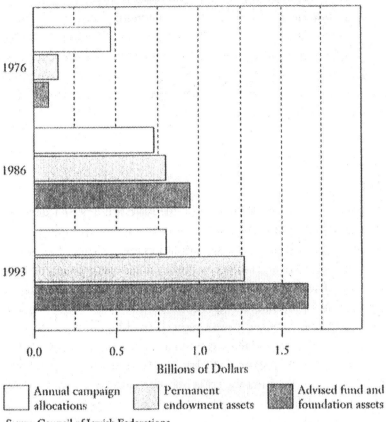

Source: Council of Jewish Federations

Research by the Planned Giving and Foundations Relations Department of the Council of Jewish Federations has found some unusual and promising patterns in the endowment market. Among annual donors of under $10,000, there appears to be little correlation between the size of the gift to the annual campaign and the propensity to make a major endowment or its actual size. In fact, 32 percent of major endowment donors in the years 1983 to 1988 gave less than $100 annually but their median endowment gift was nearly $200,000. Since women usually outlive men the "women's angle" is crucial in developing this market. Of major ($50,000 plus) endowment commitments to federations, women accounted for 36 percent with the remainder given either by men or couples. Thirty-seven percent of the gifts came from women donating under $100 to the campaign compared with 7 percent who donated over $10,000 annually. Childlessness, not current giving level, was the best predictor of endowment commitment. Fewer than 20 percent of elderly Jewish women are childless but they account for 80 percent of the major endowment gifts received from women.

Conclusion

In light of changes and trends, both the American Jewish leadership and the Israelis agree that the emphasis for American Jews today should turn toward resisting assimilation and securing their long-term viability. Raising children as Jews is a necessary prerequisite to raising dollars for Jewish causes. Moreover, there is a general consensus that fundraising and giving are tools for Jewish involvement and betterment, not ends in themselves. The new buzz word is "Jewish continuity," which means an investment in Jewish identity-building processes, particularly Jewish education and trips to Israel for young people. Whether this plan for cultural renewal will be successful is a question that will take at least a generation to answer. But the emphasis on inner rather than outer directions seems in keeping with the *zeitgeist*.

We shall soon learn whether it is as possible to inspire people to raise large amounts of funds in order to erase cultural and spiritual deprivation as it was to fight social deprivation and anti-Semitism. A successful outcome will have wider merit than just for Jewish philanthropy alone. The Jewish tradition has long proven to be an important motivator for altruism. Maintaining a significant portion of Judaically aware and educated people within the urban professional and managerial classes will probably be a positive influence on even the national culture of giving.

References

Kosmin, B. A. "The Political Economy of Gender in Jewish Federations." *Contemporary Jewry*, Spring 1989, *10* (1), 17–31.

Kosmin, B. A., and Ritterband, P. *Contemporary Jewish Philanthropy in America*. Savage, Md.: Rowman and Littlefield, 1991.

Kosmin, B. A., Goldstein, S., Waksberg, J., Lerer, N. Keyser, A., and Scheckner, J. *Highlights of the CJF National Jewish Population Survey*. New York: Council of Jewish Federations, 1991.

Tobin, G. A. *Israel and the Changing Character of Fundraising*. Research Report, no. 11. Waltham, Mass.: Maurice and Marilyn Cohen Center for Modern Jewish Studies, Brandeis University, 1994.

BARRY A. KOSMIN *is director of the Mandell L. Berman Institute at the City University of New York Graduate School and University Center, and director of research for the Council of Jewish Federations, New York City.*

The Asian American community is made up of many different cultural subgroups, all of which deal in different ways with tradition, separatism, and assimilation. Recent surveys are dispelling misconceptions about Asian American giving, suggesting fundraising strategies, and providing a framework for further research.

Asian American giving: Issues and challenges (A practitioner's perspective)

Stella Shao

THE 1990 population census indicates a dramatic shift in the demographics of U.S. society. Asian Americans have almost doubled their numbers in each of the past three decades: presently estimated at 7.3 million compared with 250,000 in 1940, they are the fastest growing segment of the U.S. population. Based on recent trends, this population is projected to total about 20 million by the year 2020. At the present time, most Asian Americans reside in five states: Hawaii, California, Illinois, New York, and Texas.

This growth has tremendous implications for various aspects of American life, including the institution of philanthropy and its other side—fundraising. Asian Americans are no longer "invisible" and no longer "insulated" from American institutions. Hence, it is appropriate for all Americans, Asians and non-Asians alike, to learn

NEW DIRECTIONS FOR PHILANTHROPIC FUNDRAISING, NO. 8, SUMMER 1995 © JOSSEY-BASS PUBLISHERS

as much as we can of one another and to understand both the similarities and the differences between Asian American groups.

Asian American diversity

Composed of more than twenty different ethnic subgroups, the Asian American community is one of the most diverse and complex minority groups in the nation. The following list identifies major Asian groups and Pacific Islander groups.

Asian Groups, by Ethnicity	Pacific Islander Groups, by Ethnicity
Chinese	Polynesian
Filipino	Hawaiian
Japanese	Samoan
Asian Indian	Tongan
Korean	Other Polynesian
Vietnamese	Micronesian
Cambodian	Guamanian
Hmong	Other Micronesian
Laotian	Melanesian
Thai	Other Pacific Islander
Other Asians	

Asians speak different languages, practice different religions, observe different customs and traditions, and come from native countries with very different histories and cultures.

Even within each language there are many different dialects, and even within each tradition there are varied cultural values and practices. However, the Census Bureau and marketing and academic surveys often consider Asian and Pacific Islander (API) Americans as one ethnic group. This technique has created stereotypes and perpetuated misperceptions about API groups in the mind of mainstream America. (The most prevalent of these misperceptions is the concept of the Asian American "model minority." As a whole, Asian

Americans are perceived to be hardworking, diligent achievers, who are willing to accept their lot without complaints.)

In order to appreciate the diversity of Asian Americans as well as the differences in attitudes and values among different generations of the same ethnic group, it is critical to understand the historical experience of each of the ethnic groups in America. Most of the first generation of Asian Americans came to America in the 1800s. They were primarily from China, Japan, and the Philippines. They came here as manual laborers who built railroads, cultivated farmland, and worked as domestic help in private homes. The second wave of Asian Americans immigrated to the United States after the elimination of racially biased immigration quotas in 1965. They were primarily professionals, technicians, students, and business people. Finally, with the fall of Cambodia, Laos, and Vietnam in 1975, there was a massive exodus from these three countries, resulting in the admission of an unprecedented number of Asian refugees into the United States. Each wave of immigrants differs from the others in its socioeconomic and educational profile. Each brings with it different skills and resources, resulting in different needs and contributions. However, all these immigrants experienced some kind of prejudice and racism in America.

Depending on the historical experience of each of the Asian ethnic groups in America, there are different degrees of separatism from or assimilation into the mainstream European American culture. For example, Chinese Americans were the earliest and the largest wave of Asian immigrants to arrive in the United States. They experienced some of the most hostile and punitive practices. Retreating into their own communities, they formed chinatowns, which functioned as complex and self-sufficient networks created for survival and community development. The internment of Japanese Americans during World War II had a different impact on that group. Paradoxically, being accused of being un-American because of their ancestry forced a quicker and more thorough assimilation of Japanese Americans into the American culture. It promoted more participation in the American political arena but also left Japanese Americans more cautious and less aggressive about retaining their own traditional practices.

Asian American culture of giving

The word *culture* may be defined as a dynamic, creative, and continuous process. It includes behaviors, values, and ways of thinking and reacting that help guide people and give meaning to their lives. In spite of the differences among the ethnic groups that comprise the Asian American community, it is critical to note that in all East Asian countries teachings from Buddhism, Confucianism, and Taoism are at the root of the culture. These traditions have become so integrated into the way people live that often Asians themselves are not aware of the origins of their values. For example, from Buddha we have learned the value of compassion and service to others; from Confucius we have understood the concepts of "benevolence" and "filial piety" and the importance of rituals in human affairs; from Lao Tzu through the Tao Teh Chin, we have acquired the perception of the "relatedness of all things," the cyclical nature of change and the reciprocity that characterizes all human relationships.

The Asian American culture of giving can, thus, be seen as an integral part of everyday life. It is based on commonly held beliefs in the value of compassion, the importance of relationships with families and communities, and in the reciprocity of gift-giving and relating, ceremonially and ritualistically carried out at each occasion throughout life. Philanthropy as such is not considered a separate and categorical concept. Asians give because of their understanding that benevolence, compassion, interdependence, and basic respect for humankind are necessary ingredients to living, first in their families, then in their own ethnic communities, and then in the greater society. Detailed examples have been wonderfully illustrated in *Ethnic Philanthropy* by Smith, Shue, Vest, and Villarreal (1994).

Compared with those of mainstream America, giving practices among Asian Americans are more focused, ethnic-specific, ritualistic, and institutionalized. Giving is often related to specific occasions and causes that will help preserve Asian culture and assist in the survival of Asian people in a foreign, and at times hostile, environment. To the extent that immigrant groups are isolated from participation and assimilation in the broader culture, the traditional practices of these groups will continue to be ethnic-specific and traditional. Anglo Americans historically had similar tendencies to give within ethnic-specific groups but have shifted to more general areas of interest as acculturalization and assimilation have been completed.

Asian American culture is now in transition. As Asian Americans participate more fully in American society, they are likely to become more involved in the American form of organized philanthropy. At the same time, more than ever there is great enthusiasm and commitment to preserving and strengthening one's ethnic identity and culture, which will tend to keep giving ethnic-specific. Achieving a balance between assimilation into mainstream culture and retention of one's traditional culture will continue to be a challenge for each and every immigrant group in America.

Studies on Asian American giving patterns

One common misperception about Asian Americans is that they are stingy, not a very giving or generous people. Another misperception is that all Asians are high achievers and doing well economically; thus why should they need help from the general public?

In response to these kinds of accusations, a couple of informal and geographically limited studies on Asian American giving patterns were carried out in the last decade. The first of these was Rosalyn Miyoko Tonai's paper on "Asian American Charitable Giving" (1988). Tonai surveyed 321 Asians in the San Francisco–Oakland area who had a history of giving. They gave on the average of 2.7 percent of their household income to charity. This puts them in the category of "substantial givers," defined by the Independent Sector as 2.5 percent of household income. Inspired by Tonai's research,

Elaine Ko and Danny Howe from United Way of King County in Seattle, Washington, conducted a survey of charitable giving in King County's Asian American community: "The Asian American Charitable Giving Study" (1990). Ko's findings also confirmed that Asian Americans, contrary to their own notions that Asians are not generous, are "substantial givers." Furthermore, Asian Americans in this sample did not give exclusively to Asian nonprofits but also to non-Asian causes. Indeed, health-related organizations and United Way or federated campaigns ranked as the top recipient organizations.

At the same time, groups such as the Independent Sector, United Way, and the Council on Foundations have begun to take notice of the dearth of information available on Asian Americans in general and their giving patterns in particular. The Council on Foundations launched a project on "Pluralism in Philanthropy" (1990), which resulted in Dr. Robert Lee's 1990 publication, *Guide to Chinese American Philanthropy and Charitable Giving Patterns.* As the title indicates, this is primarily a study of the largest Asian group in the United States and it is certainly not representative of all Asian Americans. To date, the broadest and perhaps the most interesting work on Asian American giving patterns may be found in *Ethnic Philanthropy* (Smith, Shue, Vest, and Villarreal, 1994), which updates an earlier 1992 study. This study presents anecdotal stories from interviews of Asians, Hispanics, and African Americans who described their traditional and present customs of sharing and giving money, goods, and services.

Although the research on the giving patterns of Asian Americans is slowly growing, it is still very limited at this time. What we know so far suggests certain ideas. Each preliminary hypothesis may not only help the majority correct common misconceptions of the Asian American culture of giving but also help fundraisers understand Asian American motivations for giving.

Asian Americans are very generous in giving and sharing. Asian Americans give more per household income than the average general population.

Asian Americans have a long tradition of gift exchange and caring for family members, extending to their ethnic communities. Any major fundraising campaign will probably be most successful if it is rooted within the community. (A recent example of this is the San Francisco library fund drive, which was designed to be ethnic-specific and has been quite successful.)

There has been an increase in the establishment of foundations and trusts among Asian Americans. This has happened in recent years, particularly among the Chinese.

Asian Americans contribute to non-Asian groups, particularly in the area of education and federated campaigns. However, perceiving the inequitable giving of mainstream America toward the needs of the Asian American communities, Asian Americans have focused on giving primarily to Asian groups.

Some very interesting preliminary demographic work has been done (see, for instance, Jacobson and Cooley, 1990; Kimura, 1990; *Asian Americans and Pacific Islanders in Philanthropy,* 1992). The recently established Asian Pacific American Community Fund in San Francisco is attempting to increase resources for Asian organizations in the Bay Area through coordinated annual fundraising with goals ranging from $600,000 to $3 million. As a first step in its market research, the Asian Pacific Fund contracted with the Asian American and Pacific Islander Health Forum to conduct an analysis of 1990 census data available on upper-income API households in five Bay Area counties. Census analysis focused on households with annual incomes in three groups: $75,000 to $99,000, $100,000 to $149,000, and $150,000 and over. The analysis looked within ethnic groups, with particular attention to Chinese, Filipino, Japanese, and Korean households, taking into account language ability, household composition, place of birth, and geography.

Key findings to date are geographically limited, but they are further proof of the important role that Asian Americans can play in philanthropy.

1. There are 49,000 Asian households in the Bay Area with annual incomes of $75,000 or more. This is roughly proportional

for all Asian households without regard to income, that is, Bay Area Asians are in higher-income households in the same proportion as they are in lower-income households. These households are distributed among Asian ethnic groups as follows (percentage distribution of all households reported in parentheses): Chinese, 42.7 percent (37.0); Filipino, 24.4 percent (26.6); Japanese, 12.5 percent (8.2); Asian Indian, 7.1 percent (5.8); Korean, 3.5 percent (4.5); Vietnamese, 5.8 percent (9.7); other/API, 4.0 percent (8.1).

2. Among API households for the Bay Area with annual incomes of $75,000 or more those who indicated that they "do not speak English well" constituted no more than 7 percent of the API higher-income group. In San Francisco, 15.9 percent do not speak English well; in San Mateo County the percentage drops to 3.0.

3. A significant number of high income API households have no children. Many of these people are in the 25 to 45 year old age range.

4. Upper-income API households with no children are usually U.S. born or immigrated before 1980. With the exception of Asian Indians and a very small number of Koreans, they seldom comprise more than 15 percent of households.

Challenges

The 1990s are an exciting decade for Asian Americans. They represent the beginning of some breakthroughs in the informational barrier that has kept us all—Asians and non-Asians alike—ignorant of critical issues facing Asian Americans. Breaking this barrier has generated information regarding Asian Americans that will be extremely useful in understanding the Asian American culture of giving and its relation to U.S. philanthropy in general. Groups such as the Asian American and Pacific Islander Health Forum, Asian and Pacific Islander Center for Census Information and Services (both with offices in San Francisco), and the Asian Pacific American Public Policy Institute, which is a Leadership Education for Asian Pacifics (LEAP) organization based in Los Angeles (*The State of Asian Amer-*

ica, 1993; Ong, 1994) to name a few, have recently been providing challenging educational and research information to Asian and non-Asian Americans alike. In turn, the breakdown of these informational barriers has allowed the inclusion of Asian Americans in political, cultural, educational, and philanthropic forums. For example, the recent surge of Asian American participation in literature, arts, politics, and current affairs has given Asians an opportunity to define and convey the Asian image themselves.

The challenges are the following: What is the potential for Asian Americans' full participation in the field of American philanthropy? What does it mean to fundraisers? Some possible answers have been suggested in the previous sections. The increasing visibility of Asian Americans in U.S. society will reveal much more in coming years. At this time, there are more questions than answers for future fundraising efforts targeted at Asian Americans. The Asian Pacific American Community Fund, in a recent search for information about fundraising targeted toward Asian Americans, looked at a number of issues, which can be used as a framework for further research.

1. *Motivation and appeal.* How important are the mainstream factors of name recognition, trust, and knowledge of the impact of a contribution for Asian Americans?

   How likely are Asian Americans to respond to the following themes?

   Obligation

   Sacrifice

   Pain and suffering of the poor

   Discrimination against Asians, social justice issues in general

   Ethnic pride through affiliation with a prestigious organization

   Educational opportunity and achievement

   A sense of community and of belonging

   Giving back to the community

   Should fundraising appeals specify individual Asian ethnic groups or can they refer generically to Asians? Are Asians likely only to give funds if they will benefit their own Asian ethnic group?

Are Asians more likely to contribute if a prominent Asian is involved or endorses the work?

2. *Access.* Because existing fund development resources and direct marketing resources have extremely limited databases that are exclusively Asian, what are the best means to locate these potential donors?

Are we more likely to gain their attention and interest through professional associations, civic groups, mainstream charities, ethnic media, mainstream media, or by following their patterns as consumers?

3. *Mechanisms.* Fundraising can be cause-oriented (flood or earthquake victim appeals), include incentives (gifts or items of cash value, like performing arts and athletic event tickets), be associational (offer membership and affinity group fees, annual pledges). Which mechanisms are most appealing to Asians?

Are Asians more likely to respond to appeals made by mail, over the telephone, or in person?

4. *Ethnic group variances.* How do the characteristics of motivation and appeal, access, and mechanisms vary by Asian ethnic group, if at all?

Conclusion

If the field of organized philanthropy is considered to be relatively young then Asian American philanthropy must still be in its infancy. As we watch and participate in the growth of American philanthropy, we would be remiss if we did not pay special attention to the support and nurturance of philanthropy within the ethnic communities. Based on the historical integration of immigrant groups, the more the dominant culture includes Asian Americans in its social, political, and economic institutions the more Asian Americans will become involved in the American style of organized philanthropy.

The challenge is bringing together both cultures to create a form of philanthropy that combines the best qualities of both East and West. Indeed, in an ideal world, giving will occur less because of ethnic devotion and more because of compassion and love for humankind.

References

Asian Americans and Pacific Islanders in Philanthropy. *Invisible and in Need: Philanthropic Giving to Asian Americans and Pacific Islanders*. A Report of Asian Americans and Pacific Islanders in Philanthropy (AAPIP). San Francisco: AAPIP, 1992.

Jacobson, D., and Cooley, A. "Charitable Behavior and Philanthropic Attitudes: Santa Clara County 1990." A publication of the Community Foundation of Santa Clara County, Calif., 1990.

Kimura, N. "A Study of Charitable Giving and Financial Support to Asian Pacific Human Service Organizations in Los Angeles." Paper commissioned by the Pacific Asian Resource Coordination Project of the Asian Pacific Planning Council Los Angeles: AAPCON, 1990.

Ko, E., and Howe, D. "The Asian American Charitable Giving Study: A Survey of Charitable Giving in King County's Asian American Community." Seattle, Wash.: United Way of King County, 1990.

Lee, R. *Guide to Chinese American Philanthropy and Charitable Giving Patterns.* San Rafael, Calif.: Pathway Press, 1990.

Lynn, K. *Pluralism In Philanthropy*. Washington, D.C.: Council on Foundations, 1990.

Ong, P. (ed.). *The State of Asian America: Economic Diversity, Issues & Policies.* Los Angeles: Leadership Education for Asian Pacifics (LEAP) Asian Pacific American Public Policy Institute and UCLA Asian American Studies Center, 1994.

Smith, B., Shue, S., Vest, J. L., and Villarreal, J. *Ethnic Philanthropy: Sharing and Giving Money, Goods, and Services in the African American, Mexican, Chinese, Japanese, Filipino, Korean, Guatemalan, and Salvadoran Communities of the San Francisco Bay Area.* San Francisco: Institute for Nonprofit Organization Management, College of Professional Studies, University of San Francisco, 1994.

The State of Asian America: Policy Issues to the Year 2020. Los Angeles: Leadership Education for Asian Pacifics (LEAP) Asian Pacific American Public Policy Institute and UCLA Asian American Studies Center, 1993.

Tonai, R. M. "Asian American Charitable Giving: An Analysis of the Relationship Between Demographic, Attitudinal, and Situational Factors and Cash Contributions of Asian Americans to Nonprofit Organizations in San Francisco-Oakland Area." San Francisco: Institute for Nonprofit Organization Management, College of Professional Studies, University of San Francisco, 1988.

STELLA SHAO *is president of Shao and Associates in Oakland, California, an affiliate of the Funding Resources Group. She was a founding board member of Asian Americans and Pacific Islanders in Philanthropy.*

Part Two

Gender and giving

The growing presence of women donors and fund-
raisers raises questions about different practices based
on gender. Whether or not differences between the
philanthropic actions of women and men really do
exist, the authors of this chapter make the case that
the qualities and priorities historically associated with
women are good for philanthropy overall.

5

Women giving money, women raising money: What difference for philanthropy?

Susan A. Ostrander, Joan M. Fisher

JOE MIXER, cofounder of The Fundraising School, writes that "women are coming to dominate the critical profession of fundraising" (Odendahl and O'Neil, 1994, p. 13) and Julie C. Conry makes the same claim (1991, p. 147). "Women in philanthropy is the hottest topic in fundraising today," claims a reviewer in a recent issue of the *Chronicle of Philanthropy* (Panas, 1994, p. 43).

The National Council for Research on Women (1994, p. 9) reports that according to the Internal Revenue Service, most of the wealth in the United States (60 percent of it) is owned by women; wealthy women are more likely than wealthy men to make charitable bequests (48 percent as opposed to 35 percent); and younger women especially are giving money to support social action causes. The National Committee for Responsive Philanthropy (1994) reports

NEW DIRECTIONS FOR PHILANTHROPIC FUNDRAISING, NO. 8, SUMMER 1995 © JOSSEY-BASS PUBLISHERS

that women overall are more likely to give to charitable organizations than men (81 percent compared to 69 percent). Mixer (1994) reports that women increased their philanthropic giving by a slight amount (2.4 percent) during a 1991 recession while men's contributions declined by just over 20 percent (p. 223).

What are the implications of the growing presence of women as donors and fundraisers for philanthropy in general and especially for the theory and practice of fundraising? A substantial body of evidence suggests that new ways of thinking about and carrying out fundraising are critically important to the future success, perhaps even survival, of nonprofits and charitable organizations (Kelly, 1994, p. 30). A survey reported in the *Nonprofit Times* in 1990, for example, reported that barely one-third of people surveyed believed that fundraisers were trustworthy. Four out of five people surveyed by the Gallup Organization (1993) said they were somewhat concerned or very concerned about the amount of money charitable organizations spend on fundraising.

There is inherent value in women's increased presence in giving and raising money. As Conry said at a 1990 Indiana University conference on fundraising: "Women have been the backbone of American philanthropy . . . [but] titles, money, and professional status have gone to men" (1991, p. 146). We certainly do not want to minimize the importance of women of every race and class gaining the recognition and respect they deserve for their fundraising activities. In this chapter, however, we focus on just one issue: how the apparent increase in women's influence carries the potential to make a positive difference for philanthropy overall.

We believe that women may now be in a position to bring about positive change in the theory and practice of giving and raising money and the ways in which fundraisers are trained and educated. Women donors and fundraisers may be able to create a greater focus, first, on the cause the money is intended to support and the importance of knowledge about that cause and, second, on the community created in the process of giving and raising money for the cause.

Both of these concepts—cause and community—emphasize the larger social context in which fundraising occurs. This emphasis represents a shift from the general emphasis today—on transferable fundraising techniques derived from such fields as marketing, communications, and promotion—to one on knowledge and understanding about philanthropic behavior, the place of nonprofit organizations in society, and the social issues they address.

Whether women's growing presence will actually bring about changes in the directions we expect depends in part on the choices women make today. The changes we foresee are by no means inevitable. As we will show, there is evidence both pro and con concerning whether women make positive change when they acquire new opportunities to do so. As Juanita Tamayo Lott said at a 1992 California conference on women and nonprofits: "Women can maintain power in the traditional sense—assuming power and status equal to that of men in the nonprofit sector. . . . Women also have the option to change the status quo" (Lott, 1994, p. 169).

Women as a force for positive change

A number of historical studies have documented how individual women have created and developed innovative and long-lasting philanthropic and other nonprofit institutions, especially ones devoted to improving the lives of women and children. (See, for example, Cott, 1987; Fisher, 1993, 1992; Higginbotham, 1993; McCarthy, 1990; Scott, 1991.) These institutions have included schools of various kinds, settlement houses, and social welfare and religious organizations. We know that women have sometimes introduced new and progressive ways of thinking and acting about the larger social causes that philanthropy exists to serve.

One instance of the progressive influence of women in philanthropy was documented by historian John Cumbler. During the nineteenth century, upper-class white women in one New England town acquired influence in local charitable organizations that existed mainly to help poor women and children. When they took over from their male counterparts, they shifted the conservative direction, moving from an emphasis on changing moral conduct as a way to alleviate poverty to an emphasis on providing substantive help, such as job training programs, day nurseries for children, better housing, better working conditions, job stability. Cumbler concluded that this shift had "a major [and positive] impact on policy [at this time]" (1980, p. 108).

The history of African American women in philanthropy includes numerous instances of work that focused on the larger social cause of making life better for blacks. Historian Darlene Clark Hine, for example, characterizes late nineteenth and early twentieth century philanthropy of this kind as helping blacks "to survive and to improve their lot by developing themselves. The goal was social change and individual empowerment" (1990, p. 72). The abilities of African American women were—and still are—also crucially important in gathering together the money and other resources that built the churches that continue to be the backbone of movements for racial liberation in the United States (Scott, 1990, pp. 6–8).

The philanthropy of African American women has historically put the emphasis on small donations from a number of women from a wide range of backgrounds. This kind of philanthropy develops interclass connections between women, who come together to work for a common cause. It also shows that anyone can be a philanthropist, not just people in a financial position to make large donations. This has become a principle of many of the new women's funds. As Tamayo Lott suggests: "The redefinition of [the term] philanthropist to include people of more modest means is one of redefining power" (1994, p. 175).

Although the evidence cited in the previous paragraphs suggests that women do bring about changes in philanthropy, both in the larger social aims of philanthropy and in the how and why of raising and giving money, there is also evidence that women may not make much difference in how and why philanthropy is practiced. It is now widely acknowledged that elite women philanthropists have not historically been a positive force for improving the lives of white work-ing-class or poor people or of people of color. Researcher Lynn Bur-bridge from Wellesley College writes: "The role of women in charity work should not be romanticized. For many middle-class and upper-class [white] women, charity work was the only arena within which they could attain power and prestige. . . . Despite their involvement in public service, many—including the more militant feminists—maintained the class and racial prejudices of the domi-nant society" (1994, p. 123; see also Hewitt, 1985, p. 315).

Indeed, after in-depth interviews with a sample of upper-class white women, Ostrander concluded in *Women of the Upper Class* (1984) that traditional upper-class philanthropy as practiced by these women contributed primarily to maintaining the power and privileges of their own class. Her argument is similar to that made by Teresa Odendahl in her controversial book *Charity Begins at Home* (1990).

Given this kind of opposing evidence, the choices we make at this juncture—when women's influence in philanthropy seems to be rising—are critically important. Women will have to decide how to use their influence and men will have to choose how they will respond to women's increasing power and how they will work with them in bringing about some of the changes we suggest. Do we have reasons for optimism?

Practitioner knowledge about women giving and raising money

A growing literature by fundraising practitioners outlines the dif-ferences that they have observed in why and how women and men give money for charitable purposes and why and how women and men raise money. Abbie von Schlegell and Joan Fisher (1993) pre-sent evidence that women give to nonprofit organizations for dif-ferent reasons than men do and in different ways. They claim that for women, the emphasis is the cause or purpose of the organization and connection to and involvement in that cause. Similarly, Sondra Shaw, codirector with Martha Taylor of the National Network on Women as Philanthropists, writes, "Women will seek to be involved first, and, if they enjoy what they are doing and observing, they will then give to the organization" (Shaw, 1993, p. 69).

Taylor writes that women donors seem less concerned than men with the status of an individual fundraiser and more concerned with that person's commitment to and knowledge of the organization (Taylor, 1993, p. 90). Taylor's observation seems to counter the oft-repeated principles that peers should raise money from peers and that "people give to people" rather than to causes. Taylor is careful, as are the other authors in the von Schlegell and Fisher volume, to acknowledge the lack of empirical research on these alleged gender differences.

We do not believe that it is important to determine whether individuals actually exhibit these gender differences consistently. Indeed, we want to urge against getting bogged down in a debate about whether these practitioners' observations are true. What is important is that a number of practitioners—mostly women and some men—are actively engaged in remaking and reorganizing the concept and practice of philanthropy. Furthermore, practitioners are saying that the qualities and priorities that have historically and traditionally been associated with women are good for philanthropy overall.

Thus, the critical point for us is that these supposed gender differences may provide a basis for changing philanthropy overall in the ways we are suggesting. What priorities for fundraising education and practice can we gain from these ideas?

Implications for fundraising education, training, and practice

Practicing philanthropy in accordance with priorities commonly associated with women has the potential to create a different and better kind of fundraising—one that is perhaps more ethical and socially responsible than the approaches most frequently used. At least some of the time, women's philanthropy focuses less on either giving or getting for donors, and more on addressing social causes and building common connections with others, especially other women (Kelly, 1994).

According to this way of thinking, good fundraising means having donors and fundraisers who are first and foremost committed to and informed about the specific cause the money is being raised for. As part of their craft, then, fundraisers should be more broadly educated about the social issues and concerns they are raising money for. This training should also include a certain level of "economic literacy" about how money is accumulated and distributed in society and how it is used—or not used—to address social concerns. Training should also emphasize the assumptions and values charitable organizations have about how money is used and toward what social ends.

A good education would also teach fundraisers about the role of the nonprofit organizations for which the money is being raised. Donors and fundraisers need to understand and be sympathetic to the organization's mission and manner of achieving it. This kind of knowledge includes an understanding of how these organizations function in relation to government and to for-profit organizations, both in the past and in the present, and the ways in which they operate (or should operate) from a different value base than the other two organizational types as a component of their legitimation.

A good education would help donors and fundraisers develop a sense of connection to one another that derives from mutual understanding, agreement, and collaboration in a common project. The transfer of resources—money—is the occasion for creating these relationships.

Indeed, we are suggesting a fundamental transformation in the philanthropist's concept of money: rather than a sign of status and power, it becomes a means for accomplishing collective action toward a shared goal. This concept represents a transformation in our understanding of the social responsibility of people who raise money (as well as those who give it).

This way of thinking is in vivid contrast to the more common point of view, which most often treats the cause for which the money is raised as a product to be sold or promoted with the techniques of selling and promotion as simply transferable skills across different causes. The philosophy we describe is also in vivid contrast to that which emphasizes using generic communication skills, making emotional appeals, and creating personal bonds between donor and solicitor regardless of what the money is being raised for or by whom.

Other writers about fundraising are advancing ideas similar to our own. Henry Rosso (1991) emphasizes the importance of integrating an organization's fundraising activities into its mission and goals. He emphasizes the importance of the donor's relationship to, interest in, and knowledge about the recipient organization's activities and philosophy.

Kathleen Kelly argues against using the amount of money raised as the standard of fundraising success (1991, 1994). She suggests that the success of a fundraising effort should be evaluated by "the impact those dollars have on the effectiveness of the organization," in other words, the larger social purpose the organization exists to serve (1991, p. 27). Kelly also cautions against using a marketing approach to fundraising that focuses on "selling" donor-consumers on how they will benefit if they make a gift. She cautions that the goal of fundraising is not to satisfy donor wants and advocates an approach to donors that emphasizes the larger social benefits of fundraising.

The task of the fundraiser, then, is not to convince, enlighten, or appeal. It is not to persuade, sell, or promote. Contrary to the standard philosophy of raising money, the donor's wants and needs are not primary. Instead, the focus is on the goal for which the money is being sought. The task of the fundraiser is to develop and nurture an understanding about the benefits to the larger community that philanthropic organizations exist to serve and the value of working together with others toward these benefits in mutually satisfying relationships (see Ostrander and Schervish, 1990, for a discussion of philanthropy as donor-recipient relation).

Guidelines for the day-to-day practice of fundraising

What guidelines does this perspective offer for the day-to-day practice of giving and raising money? In this section we close by suggesting some concrete practices for solicitors and donors.

1. *An emphasis on cause or issue.* Before becoming active in giving or raising money for a particular organization, donors and solicitors must show some interest and knowledge in the specific issue or cause the organization seeks to address.

The first goal of fundraising is to involve donors and fundraisers in the organization's work. This involvement precedes giving or raising money. Doing this may require a longer-term commitment to an organization than is sometimes presently the case.

When determining the size of a gift, solicitors and donors discuss the larger importance and value of the issue being addressed by the organization and the underlying causes of the issue. The parties may also develop a plan for learning more about the issue together on an ongoing basis.

Donors and solicitors consider carefully how and why the organization addresses the cause or issue in the way that it does. What evidence is there (or could there be) of appropriateness and effectiveness? This discussion may include an examination of the activities of governmental and for-profit organizations in addressing the same cause and of the place and value of the charitable organizations that do so. It should be noted that there is evidence that women may be especially interested in contributing to causes or raising money for organizations that seek some social change.

Solicitors and donors look at the amount and kind of societal resources available to deal with the issue or cause, including tax dollars and funds from for-profit groups. This examination could aid in the assessment of sources and priorities for acquiring and distributing philanthropic dollars.

2. *An emphasis on community and connection.* Because involvement precedes giving, relationships between solicitors and potential donors—and perhaps among donors, especially women—are built. Thus, it takes time before the solicitor asks and the donor gives.

The relationship between donor and solicitor is based on a shared commitment to and knowledge about the organization and its reason for existence. Thus, the relationship is based on content rather than emotion.

Increased donor engagement and participation in setting goals for fundraising and for the organization itself may be appropriate as part of building both community and organizational effectiveness. Ideally, the organization's beneficiaries or constituents are also involved. Fundraising staff may serve as mediating links between donors and beneficiaries or constituents.

Bringing donors together in ongoing exploration of all of these issues is a useful way to be involved in the work of the organization, including the work of raising money. This coming together of donors may also include beneficiaries or constituents.

References

Burbridge, L. "The Occupational Structure of Nonprofit Industries: Implications for Women." In T. Odendahl and M. O'Neil (eds.), *Women and Power in the Nonprofit Sector*. San Francisco: Jossey-Bass, 1994.

Conry, J. C. "The Feminization of Fundraising." In D. Burlingame and L. J. Hulse (eds.), *Taking Fundraising Seriously: Advancing the Profession and Practice of Raising Money*. San Francisco: Jossey-Bass, 1991.

Cott, N. *The Grounding of Modern Feminism*. New Haven, Conn.: Yale University Press, 1987.

Cumbler, J. "The Politics of Charity: Gender and Class in Late 19th Century Charity Policy." *Journal of Social History*, 1980, *14*, 99–111.

Fisher, J. M. "Celebrating the Heroines of Philanthropy." *Women's Philanthropy, a National Agenda, Wingspread Proceedings*. Racine: Center for Women and Philanthropy, University of Wisconsin, 1992.

Fisher, J. M. *A Study of Six Women Philanthropists of the Early Twentieth Century*. Unpublished doctoral dissertation, School of the Union Institute, Cincinnati, Ohio, 1993.

Gallup Organization. *American's Attitudes Regarding Regulation of Charitable Organizations*, Aug. 1993. (Available from the Council of Better Business Bureaus, Philanthropy Advisory Service, 4200 Wilson Boulevard, Arlington, Va.)

Hewitt, N. A. "Beyond the Search for Sisterhood: American Women's History in the 1980s." *Social History*, 1985, *10* (3), 299–321.

Higginbotham, E. B. *Righteous Discontent: The Women's Movement in the Black Baptist Church, 1880–1920*. Cambridge, Mass.: Harvard University Press, 1993.

Hine, D. C. "We Specialize in the Wholly Impossible: The Philanthropic Work of Black Women." In K. McCarthy (ed.), *Lady Bountiful Revisited: Women, Philanthropy, and Power*. New Brunswick, N.J.: Rutgers University Press, 1990.

Kelly, K. S. *Fundraising and Public Relations: A Critical Analysis*. Hillsdale, N.J.: Erlbaum, 1991.

Kelly, K. S. *Building Fund-Raising Theory: An Empirical Test of Four Models of Practice*. Essays on Philanthropy, no. 12. Indianapolis: Indiana University Center on Philanthropy, 1994.

Lott, J. T. "Women Changing Demographics, and the Redefinition of Power." In T. Odendahl and M. O'Neil (eds.), *Women and Power in the Nonprofit Sector*. San Francisco: Jossey-Bass, 1994.

McCarthy, K. (ed.) *Lady Bountiful Revisited: Women, Philanthropy, and Power*. New Brunswick, N.J.: Rutgers University Press, 1990.

Mixer, J. "Women as Professional Fundraisers." In T. Odendahl and M. O'Neil (eds.), *Women and Power in the Nonprofit Sector*. San Francisco: Jossey-Bass, 1994.

National Committee for Responsive Philanthropy. "Women and Philanthropy Analyzed, National Action Agenda Developed." *Responsive Philanthropy*. (Newsletter) Washington, D.C.: National Committee for Responsive Philanthropy, Winter 1994, p. 6.

National Council for Research on Women (New York). "Philanthropy: Do Universal Dollars Reach Women and Girls?" *Issues Quarterly*, 1994, *1* (2).

Odendahl, T. *Charity Begins at Home: Generosity and Self-Interest Among the Philanthropic Elite*. New York: Basic Books, 1990.

Odendahl, T., and O'Neil, M. (eds.). *Women and Power in the Nonprofit Sector*. San Francisco: Jossey-Bass, 1994.

Ostrander, S. A. *Women of the Upper Class*. Philadelphia: Temple University Press, 1984.

Ostrander, S. A., and Schervish, P. G. "Giving and Getting: Philanthropy as Social Relation." In J. Van Til and Associates (eds.), *Critical Issues in American Philanthropy: Strengthening Theory and Practice*. San Francisco: Jossey-Bass, 1990.

Panas, J. "Are Women Donors Really That Different from Men?" *Chronicle of Philanthropy*, Feb. 8, 1994, p. 43.

Rosso, H. A., and Associates. *Achieving Excellence in Fundraising*. San Francisco: Jossey-Bass, 1991.

Scott, A. F. "Most Invisible of All: Black Women's Voluntary Associations." *Journal of Southern History*, 1990, *56* (1), 3–22.

Scott, A. F. *Natural Allies: Women's Associations in American History*. Champaign: University of Illinois Press, 1991.

Shaw, S. C. "Communicating with Women: Understanding and Applying Differences." In A. J. von Schlegell and J. M. Fisher (eds.), *Women as Donors, Women as Philanthropists*. New Directions for Philanthropic Fundraising, no. 2. San Francisco: Jossey-Bass, 1993.

Taylor, M. "Training Women to Seek Major Gifts." In A. J. von Schlegell and J. M. Fisher (eds.), *Women as Donors, Women as Philanthropists*. New Directions for Philanthropic Fundraising, no. 2. San Francisco: Jossey-Bass, 1993.

Von Schlegell, A. J., and Fisher, J. M. (eds.). *Women as Donors, Women as Philanthropists*. New Directions for Philanthropic Fundraising, no. 2. San Francisco: Jossey-Bass, 1993.

SUSAN A. OSTRANDER *is professor of sociology at Tufts University in Medford, Massachusetts, and author of* Women of the Upper Class.

JOAN M. FISHER *is deputy director of B'nai B'rith Women of Washington, D.C., and managing partner of the consulting firm of James L. Fisher, Ltd.*

Part Three

Major factors influencing giving

By looking at both income and wealth, the authors show that generosity does not vary much by income, present the first systematic findings on wealth and philanthropy, and offer important practical implications for fundraising.

6

Wherewithal and beneficence: charitable giving by income and wealth

Paul G. Schervish, John J. Havens

IT IS OUR contention that taking fundraising seriously requires a serious analysis of the data about the donors to whom fundraisers appeal. In this chapter we review three sets of research findings on the relationship between philanthropic giving and levels of income and wealth. These findings derive from research conducted by us at the Boston College Social Welfare Research Institute, which was graciously supported over the past few years by the Indiana University Center on Philanthropy, the Lilly Endowment, and the T. B. Murphy Foundation. In the first section of the chapter we discuss the relationship between level of income and percentage of income donated to charity. In the second section we explore the relationship between wealth and the percentages of income and wealth donated to charity. In the third section we summarize some relevant preliminary findings on giving and household finances. We

NEW DIRECTIONS FOR PHILANTHROPIC FUNDRAISING, NO. 8, SUMMER 1995 © JOSSEY-BASS PUBLISHERS

conclude with a discussion of the major empirical findings and their implication for fundraising.

Do the poor pay more?

We review the relationship between income and philanthropic giving from two perspectives (see Schervish and Havens, 1995). We begin by looking at the magnitude of philanthropic contributions made by various income groups, using four macromeasures of giving patterns averaged over groups of households. Then we present findings from micro, individual-household data to convey the relationship between household gross income and the percentage of that income contributed to philanthropy. We show where the "U-shaped" relationship, which is frequently construed as evidence that the poor pay more than the wealthy, comes from. We then go on to recalculate the relationship between income and giving, showing why in general the data do not support the contention that the poor pay more (in the sense of contributing a greater percentage of their income to philanthropy). The findings are based on statistical analysis of a data set we constructed by combining data from the 1990 (reporting contributions for 1989) and 1992 (reporting contributions for 1991) national surveys of giving and volunteering in the United States conducted by the Gallup Organization for the Independent Sector (Hodgkinson and Weitzman, 1990; with Noga and Gorski, 1992). For more information on how we constructed this data set, see Schervish and Havens, 1992.

The central question is whether the conventional notion that the poor are more generous than the wealthy is indeed correct. In other words, is what Stanley Salett (in Schervish and others, 1993, p. 78) reads and reports actually true? That is, the Independent Sector (IS) data show "that the less affluent were more generous than the very wealthy." For starters, we point out that the Independent Sector data cannot provide any answers to questions about the generosity of the rich and the poor. We must turn to other sources to obtain such information, as we shall discuss in the second major section of this chapter. For now it is important to point out that the Independent Sector data to which Salett refers and on which we base the analysis in this section provides information only on *household income*. Hence, while we can compare *upper- and lower-income households*, we cannot use the data to compare *wealthy and poor households*.

Four macromeasures of contribution by income level

In this section, we analyze contribution data for each of the thirteen categories of gross household income (Table 6.1). The analysis answers four questions about the relative magnitude of contributions by households at different income levels.

1. How much do households at different income levels contribute to philanthropy? Households in the upper five income categories ($40,000 or more in 1991 dollars) contributed 65 percent (or $45.6 billion) of the total reported contributions in 1989 and 66 percent (or $40.7 billion) of the total reported contributions in 1991. Households in the bottom eight income categories contributed 35 percent (or $24.7 billion) of the total reported contributions in 1989 and 34 percent (or $20.5 billion) of the total reported contributions in 1991 (see Table 6.1, Panels 2 and 4 for details by income category).

Figure 6.1 graphically presents the finding that lower income levels contribute far less in absolute terms than do higher income categories. (We should point out that the charts based on combined data adjust income categories for inflation between 1989 and 1991 on an individual record basis while the charts reporting aggregate figures separately for each year adjust income categories for inflation on an aggregate basis. The generally small discrepancies between the two methods do not result in changes in the general shapes and patterns which are the subject of discussion in this paper.)

2. What is the average contribution of households at different income levels? The average contribution per household rises from $79 in 1989 and $114 in 1991 for households earning less than $7,000 per year to about twenty times as much ($1,963 in 1989 and $2,208 in 1991) for households earning $100,000 or more (see Table 6.1,

Table 6.1. Selected Measures of Contribution for Households, 1989 and 1991

Panel	Year	Under $7,000	$7,000–$9,999	$10,000–$14,999	$15,000–$19,999	$20,000–$24,999	$25,000–$29,999	$30,000–$34,999	$35,000–$39,999	$40,000–$49,999	$50,000–$59,999	$60,000–$74,999	$75,000–$99,999	$100,000– or more	Total
1. Sample Size															
	1989	137	137	180	211	205	198	197	151	213	208	213	124	79	2253
	1991	150	98	149	156	180	180	171	183	189	212	219	123	102	2112
2. Total Annual Contributions (billions of 1991 dollars)															
	1989	0.3	1.0	2.4	2.5	4.2	4.6	5.0	4.8	7.3	6.8	8.7	12.2	10.6	70.4
	1991	0.8	0.8	1.8	4.0	3.0	3.7	3.3	3.2	6.4	7.9	9.1	8.8	8.5	61.3
3. Average Dollar Contribution per Household															
	1989	79	298	383	397	700	661	894	698	858	1,019	1,289	2,468	1,963	863
	1991	114	149	243	508	410	522	570	517	917	1,201	1,314	1,751	2,208	734
4. Cumulative Annual Contribution (percentage)															
	1989	0.5	2.0	5.4	8.9	14.9	21.4	28.5	35.4	45.8	55.4	67.7	85.0	100.0	100.0
	1991	1.4	2.6	5.5	12.0	16.9	22.9	28.3	33.5	44.0	56.9	71.7	86.2	100.0	100.0
5. Cumulative Percentage of Households															
	1989	5.5	11.0	19.5	27.9	37.1	45.9	54.1	61.6	72.5	81.0	89.4	95.6	100.0	100.0
	1991	8.9	15.1	23.8	33.3	41.9	50.4	57.4	64.8	73.1	81.1	89.3	95.4	100.0	100.0
6. Percentage of Contribution															
	1989	0.5	1.5	3.4	3.6	5.9	6.5	7.1	6.9	10.4	9.6	12.3	17.3	15.0	100.0
	1991	1.4	1.3	2.9	6.5	4.8	6.0	5.4	5.2	10.4	13.0	14.8	14.4	13.8	100.0
7. Percentage of Total Income															
	1989	0.8	1.3	2.8	3.9	5.5	6.2	7.0	7.3	12.9	12.1	14.6	14.0	11.7	100.0
	1991	1.3	1.4	3.0	4.4	5.3	6.3	6.2	7.5	10.3	11.9	15.3	14.5	12.6	100.0
8. Share of Contribution per Share of Income															
	1989	0.60	1.17	1.22	0.92	1.08	1.04	1.02	0.94	0.81	0.79	0.85	1.24	1.28	1.00
	1991	1.10	0.87	0.97	1.47	0.91	0.95	0.87	0.69	1.02	1.09	0.97	1.00	1.10	1.00

Household Income

Source: Social Welfare Research Institute at Boston College analysis of data from Independent Sector's *Survey of Giving and Volunteering in the United States*

Figure 6.1. Annual Philanthropic Contributions, by Household Income

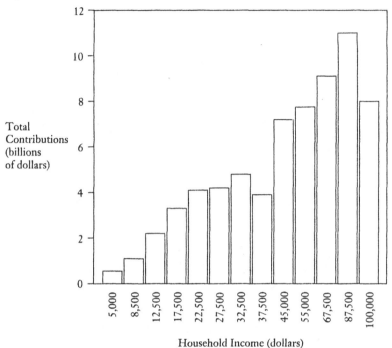

Household Income (dollars)

Source: Social Welfare Research Institute at Boston College analysis of combined 1989 and 1991 data from Independent Sector's *Survey of Giving and Volunteering in the United States*

Panel 3). Figure 6.2 presents this information in graphic form. Once again, the average contribution per household is strongly skewed, with upper-income households donating substantially larger amounts than lower-income households.

3. What percentage of total contributions is made by the households in the highest income quintile as compared with those in the lowest income quintile? In 1989 the 20 percent of households with the lowest incomes (less than $15,800 annually) contributed 5.7 percent of total contributions while the 20 percent of households with the highest incomes ($49,020 or above) contributed 45.6 percent of the total. Similarly, in 1991 the 20 percent of households with the lowest incomes (less than $12,815) contributed 4.2 percent of contributions while the 20 percent of households with the highest

Figure 6.2. Average Household Contribution, by Household Income

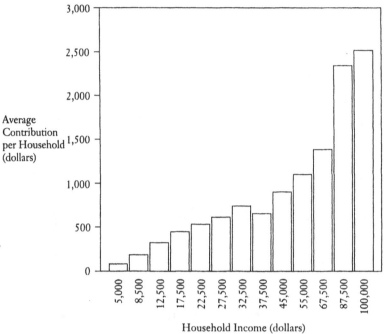

Household Income (dollars)

Source: Social Welfare Research Institute at Boston College analysis of combined 1989 and 1991 data from Independent Sector's *Survey of Giving and Volunteering in the United States*

incomes ($48,675 or above) contributed approximately 44.5 percent (see Table 6.1, Panels 4 and 5). In passing, it is interesting to note that Panel 5 shows that over half the households earn less than $35,000 in annual gross household income (1991 dollars) as reported in the IS survey data. This is consistent with U.S. Bureau of the Census estimates of $30,126 median money income for households in 1991 (*Statistical Abstract of the United States*, 1993, Table 711, p. 457).

Figure 6.3 presents a Lorenz-type curve for philanthropic contributions. This type of curve is often used to describe the level of inequality in the national distribution of income. Here we use it to measure the degree of inequality in the national distribution of contributions as compared with the distribution of households, ordered by income. The horizontal axis measures the cumulative

Figure 6.3. Cumulative Distribution of Contributions Versus Cumulative Distribution of Households

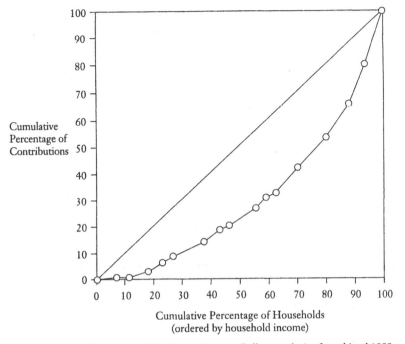

Cumulative Percentage of Contributions

Cumulative Percentage of Households
(ordered by household income)

Source: Social Welfare Research Institute at Boston College analysis of combined 1989 and 1991 data from Independent Sector's *Survey of Giving and Volunteering in the United States*

percent of households (ordered from lowest to highest household income) and the vertical axis measures the cumulative percent of total contributions made by those households. The curve identifies the percent of total contributions contributed by a designated percent of the households. Just as income is unequally distributed in the population so too are philanthropic contributions. Combining the 1989 and 1991 data, we find that the 42 percent of households with the lowest incomes (less than $25,000 annual household income) contribute approximately 16 percent of the total while the 9 percent of households with the highest incomes ($75,000 or above) contribute approximately 28 percent of the total. The higher-income households, therefore, contribute substantially more than the proportion of such households in the population.

When measured by cumulative distributions, lower-income households contribute less than higher-income households.

4. How does this cited share of total contributions made by each income category compare with its share of total income? To this end we have examined the distribution of contributions without regard to the distribution of income or the ability to pay. Lower-income households by definition have less income to contribute than do higher-income households. Thus, a complete picture of the distribution of contributions requires an additional measure that also takes household income into account. One such measure is the ratio of the percentage of total contributions made by each income group relative to the percentage of total income earned by that group. A ratio greater than one indicates that the share of contributions is larger than the share of income while a ratio of less than one indicates the reverse. For example, a share score of 1.28 for households earning $100,000 or more in 1989 indicates that these households contributed 28 percent more of the contributions than their share of income. On the other hand a score of .60 for households earning less than $7,000 in 1989 indicates that these households contributed 40 percent less of the contributions than their share of income.

Table 6.1, Panel 8 indicates a rough equality of contribution scores for 1989 and 1991 in both the lower and higher income categories and a modest tendency for households in middle income categories to contribute less than their share of income. Figure 6.4 demonstrates in graphic form the same general conclusion that there is relatively little difference in the share score among income groups. We can see that lowest income households (below $7,000) contribute the smallest share of contributions compared with their share of income. The next four income categories contribute more (about 5 to 15 percent more) than their share of income. However, the highest income households (above $80,000) contribute the greatest share (about 15 to 20 percent more) compared with their share of income. It is the group of households in the middle income range ($30,000 to $80,000) that contributes somewhat less (about 1 to 10 percent) than their share of income, with the exception of

Figure 6.4. Share of Total Contributions per Share of Total Income, by Household Income

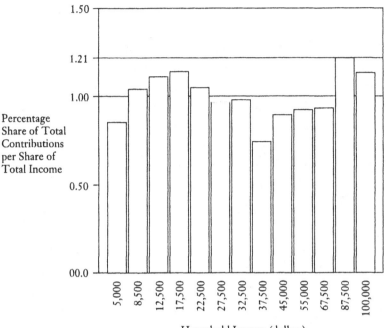

Source: Social Welfare Research Institute at Boston College analysis of combined 1989 and 1991 data from Independent Sector's *Survey of Giving and Volunteering in the United States*

households with incomes of $35,000 to $40,000, which contribute 25 percent less than their share of income. When measured by share of total contribution per share of total income, we find some disproportionate generosity in both lower- and upper-income groups. But the general tendency across all income groups is for there to be a relatively equal level of generosity rather than greater generosity only among lower-income households.

The imagery of stingy upper-income households and generous lower-income households is not sustained in the foregoing macro-analysis of the data. More than two-thirds of total contributions (more than $40 billion) are made by the top one-quarter of households. On average, households at higher income levels make contributions that are an order of magnitude larger than that of households at lower levels. The highest income quintile contributes more than ten times the amount of the lowest income quintile. On all of the first three absolute measures, higher-income households contribute many times more than lower-income households. On the fourth measure, which compares share of contributions to share of income, there is a rough equality of generosity among all income groups, with at most a modest tendency for middle-income households to contribute less than their share of income. There is no evidence to support the popular notion of caring lower-income and uncaring upper-income households. Both groups appear equally caring.

Micromeasures of contribution by household income

The Independent Sector's biennial Gallup survey also enables us to analyze the giving patterns of individual households by construct- ing three important micro measures. The first is the U-shaped pat- tern of giving that emerges when we exclude noncontributing households and look only on the subset of households that make a charitable contribution. The second is the participation rate of each income group, that is, the proportion of households in an income group that makes at least $1 in charitable contributions during the survey year. The third instructive measure is the percentage of income contributed by each income group when all (contributing and noncontributing) households are included in the statistics.

Where the U-shaped curve comes from. The first step is to reproduce the often-cited U-shaped relationship between income and giving. Table 6.2 (Panels 1 and 2) presents the data that is graphed on Figure 6.5.

Figure 6.5, like the following two figures, plots the data for con- tributions in 1989 and 1991 on the same figure because income and contributions are both adjusted to 1991 dollars. The points on the figure represent the average percentage of household gross income contributed by household income for each year. All of these averages are based on more than one hundred households (see Table 6.1,

Table 6.2. Percentage of Household Income Contributed, 1989 and 1991

Household Income (nominal dollars)

Panel	Year	Under $7,000	$7,000–$9,999	$10,000–$14,999	$15,000–$19,999	$20,000–$24,999	$25,000–$29,999	$30,000–$34,999	$35,000–$39,999	$40,000–$49,999	$50,000–$59,999	$60,000–$74,999	$75,000–$99,999	$100,000 or more
1. Household Income in 1991 Real Dollars (plotted on x-axis)														
	1989	5,357	9,107	13,392	18,749	24,106	29,463	34,820	40,177	48,212	58,926	72,318	93,746	107,138
	1991	5,000	8,500	12,500	17,500	22,500	27,500	32,500	37,500	45,000	55,000	67,500	87,500	100,000
2. Annual Average Percentage of Income Contributed, Contributing Households Only														
	1989	3.0	4.7	4.3	2.9	3.2	3.0	2.9	2.2	2.1	2.1	2.2	3.4	3.1
	1991	5.0	3.4	3.0	4.3	2.5	2.7	2.4	1.6	2.4	2.5	2.1	2.3	2.3
3. Rate of Participation in Giving (percentage of all households)														
	1989	46.6	58.1	64.9	67.7	82.3	75.1	83.9	84.2	88.8	84.7	91.4	95.5	90.2
	1991	42.9	51.0	65.2	68.1	72.7	73.0	72.5	84.2	84.7	88.6	91.1	89.0	95.6
4. Annual Average Percentage of Income Contributed, All Households														
	1989	1.4	2.7	2.8	2.0	2.6	2.2	2.4	1.8	1.8	1.8	2.0	3.2	2.8
	1991	2.2	1.8	1.9	3.0	1.8	2.0	1.8	1.4	2.0	2.2	2.0	2.0	2.2

Source: See Table 6.1.

Figure 6.5. Percentage of Household Income Contributed, by Household Income

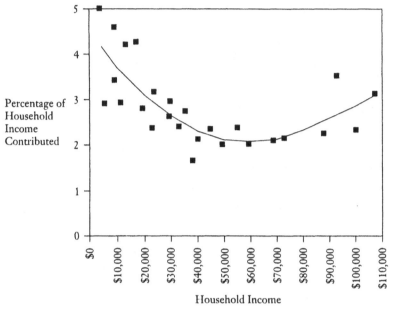

Source: Social Welfare Research Institute at Boston College analysis of combined 1989 and 1991 data from Independent Sector's *Survey of Giving and Volunteering in the United States*

Panel 1). The U-shaped curved line in Figure 6.5 is a third order polynomial that has been estimated from the data using ordinary least squares regression. It shows the trend relationship in the data and is statistically different from a horizontal line (representing no difference by income) at a .01 level of significance. The left end of the curve is higher than the right end, indicating that lower-income households contribute a greater proportion of their income than do higher-income households. The low portion of the U indicates that middle-income people give less than both lower- and higher-income households. Thus even those who cite this relationship misconstrue its content when they say they say that low- and middle-income households give a greater percentage of their incomes than upper-income households.

It might appear from this reconstruction that there is evidence that the poor do pay more. However, when we look more closely at the procedures for analyzing these data we find a critical flaw, namely, the treatment of the subpopulation of contributors as if it were the entire population. The U-shaped curve describes only those households in each income category that make a contribution and ignores all other households that contribute nothing. As such, the data describe just those who report making contributions rather than all the lower-income, all the middle-income, or all the higher-income households.

We now arrive at the key finding that sets the record straight about the so-called U-shaped curve concept, namely, that lower-income households are more likely than upper-income households to make no charitable contribution. Were there roughly equal proportions of households making contributions in each income group, the U-shaped pattern would be maintained for the population as a whole, albeit shifted downward. However, the combined data for both survey years show that the participation rates are substantially lower and statistically significant ($p < .01$) for lower-income households than for higher-income households, ranging from under 66 percent for the three lowest income groups to over 88 percent for the three highest income groups (see Table 6.2, Panel 3). As we can see from Figure 6.6, the participation rates for each income category and the least squares (logarithmic) trend curve for participation data in 1989 and 1991 show an increasing level of participation as income rises.

Recalculating the relationship for all households. The difference in participation rates implies that the relationship between income and percentage of income contributed in the population as a whole is different from that represented by the often-cited U-shaped curve. When we include all households in the analysis (Table 6.2, Panel 4), the U-shaped curve (Figure 6.5 and the upper curve in Figure 6.7) is flattened to the wavy, relatively flat curved line depicted by the lower curve in Figure 6.7. This curve is not statistically significant (even at the .2 level), that is, it is not different from a horizontal straight line. Thus we can conclude that households at all income levels contribute roughly the same percentage of their incomes to philanthropy even though there is an upturn at the right side.

Discussion. Like the macro-level analysis, the micro-level analysis

Figure 6.6. Rates of Participation, by Household Income

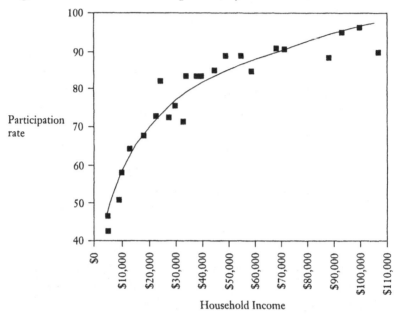

Source: Social Welfare Research Institute at Boston College analysis of combined 1989 and 1991 data from Independent Sector's *Survey of Giving and Volunteering in the United States*

does not support the contention that lower-income households donate a higher percentage of their income to charity than upper-income households. When taking into account both contributing and non-contributing households, the percentage of gross income contributed to philanthropy is roughly the same at all income levels.

However, the original U-shaped curve does tell us something important about differences in the underlying pattern of giving for lower- and upper-income households. First, many at lower-income levels contribute nothing while nearly all at upper-income levels contribute something. Second, those who do contribute at the lower end give on average a greater share of their incomes than do contributors at the upper end. Our major conclusion is that generosity is not strongly related to income and, hence, must be related to other social and personal characteristics that cut across the financial spectrum. Ferreting out some of these positive and perhaps class-blind

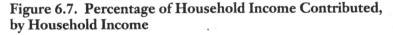

Figure 6.7. Percentage of Household Income Contributed, by Household Income

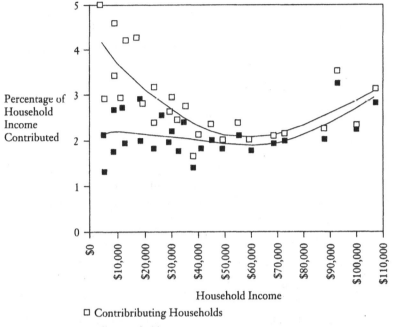

□ Contribributing Households

■ All Households

Source: Social Welfare Research Institute at Boston College analysis of combined 1989 and 1991 data from Independent Sector's *Survey of Giving and Volunteering in the United States*

sources of generosity rather than perpetuating an invidious imagery, is the task we undertake in the third section of this chapter.

Higher income, wealth, and giving

This section of the chapter presents significant findings from our current ongoing research. It is based on giving behavior from our quantitative analyses of the 1989 *Survey of Consumer Finances* (SCF). This is a representative survey of approximately twenty-seven hundred households with an oversample of approximately three hundred high-income households. The survey was conducted by the Survey

Research Center at the University of Michigan for the Federal Reserve. Our analysis has three primary objectives: (1) to confirm and extend our earlier findings regarding the relationship between household income and charitable giving; (2) to explore the relationship between household wealth and percent of income given; and (3) to discuss the problems that arise when attempting to uncover patterns in the percent of wealth contributed.

Confirmation and extension of prior findings

The 1989 SCF provides detailed information for 1988 on total annual contributions in excess of $500 as well as on household income. These data allow an independent reevaluation of the relationship between giving behavior and household income. The reevaluation graphically presented in Figure 6.8 confirms the findings cited in the previous section of this chapter for households with incomes under $100,000, with the exception that where the IS data indicate an average household contribution of 2 percent across income levels, the SCF data indicate an average contribution of 1.5 percent. We believe this discrepancy is the result of two factors. The SCF excludes contributions of less than $500 and it excludes political contributions, which we included in our analysis of the IS data. The downward curving left tail of the SCF data line reflects the fact that households that gave less than $500 in the survey year are treated as not having made a contribution. When we eliminate contributions of under $500 from the IS data to make it parallel with the SCF data, the left tail of the IS data line looks like the left tail of the SCF data line in Figure 6.8.

Although the IS survey does not support analysis beyond income of $100,000, the SCF does because of its unique oversample of more than three hundred very high income households. Figure 6.9 presents the analysis of this extended income range. The figure shows that there is a rather sharp increase in the percentage of income contributed as income increases. Charitable contributions are slightly less than 2 percent of income at $100,000, increase to approximately 3.6 percent at the $100,000 to $150,000 level, and jump to approximately 4.9 percent at the level of $1 million or more.

Figure 6.8. Percentage of Income Contributed, by Household Income Under $100,000 for All Households in the Independent Sector Data and in the *Survey of Consumer Finances*

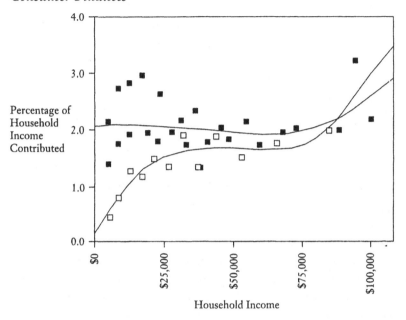

Household Income

■ All Households IS Data

□ All Households SCF Data

Note: The SCF records contributions of $500 or more annually; IS includes contributions of all amounts. Thus, (i) the average value of percentage of household income contributed is approximately 2 percent based on the IS data but is approximately 1.5 percent based on the SCF data; (ii) the plotted points based on households in the lower income range of the SCF are especially low relative to the corresponding points based on households in the lower income range of the IS data.

The curve based on IS data is not statistically significantly different from a horizontal line at the .01 significance level. The curve based on SCF data is significantly different from a horizontal line at the .05 significance level because of households in the lowest two income categories; an additional consequence of the differences discussed in the paragraph above.

The IS data combine data from the 1990 and 1992 *Survey of Giving and Volunteering in the United States*. The SCF data were collected in the 1989 survey.

If the IS data are recalculated by considering total household contributions less than $500 to be 0, similar to the SCF, the data plots become nearly identical, even in the lower income range.

Sources: Social Welfare Research Institute at Boston College analysis of combined 1989 and 1991 data from Independent Sector's *Survey of Giving and Volunteering in the United States* and 1988 data from the Federal Reserve's *Survey of Consumer Finances*

Our earlier findings must therefore be modified. In terms of the percentage of income contributed, the very affluent (households with incomes greater than $100,000) are more than twice as generous as lower- and middle-income households. Importantly, the increased percentage of income contributed at the upper-income levels is attributable primarily to a small fraction (less than 20 percent) of households in each income category that make very large contributions while the remaining households in the category make modest contributions averaging approximately 2 percent of their income (see again Figure 6.9). One possible explanation for this pattern is that higher-income households may regularly contribute a "normal" amount averaging 2 percent per year but once or twice a decade make an additional, substantial contribution.

Wealth and charitable giving

At this point in the chapter, we have discussed the relationship between household income and percent of income contributed to charity. The second set of findings from our analysis of SCF explores the relationship between wealth and giving behavior. Although much philanthropic literature speaks of differences between the rich and the poor, it is not accurate to do so on the basis of analysis of household giving behavior by income. As we have already indicated, the financial data for classifying households in our analysis of the IS data was income, not wealth.

Fortunately, the *Survey of Consumer Finances* enables us to begin to remedy this situation because it allows us to estimate the percentage of income contributed by households at different levels of net worth. As our measure of wealth, we utilized the concept of net worth, that is, all household assets minus all household liabilities. (As already noted, the SCF collects no information concerning contributions totaling less than $500 per year. So unless otherwise specified, all references to average contributions, participation rates, and percentages of income contributed are to contributions in excess of $500.) The relationship between wealth and giving is complex and requires further analysis. For our purposes here, there are several preliminary findings in Table 6.3.

Figure 6.9. Percentage of Income Contributed, by Household Income, for All Households in the *Survey of Consumer Finances*

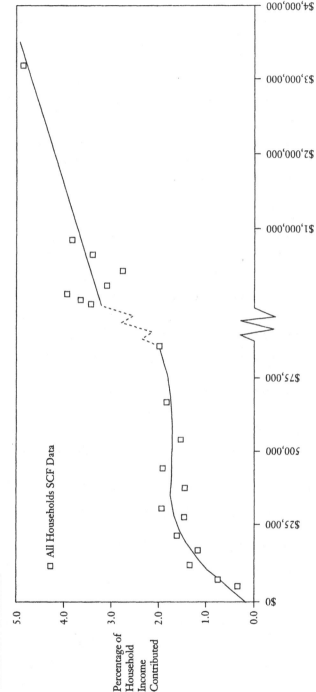

Household Income

Note: The *Survey of Consumer Finances* records contributions of $500 or more annually. On the horizontal axis, each tic to the left of the saw tooth represents $5,000 in 1988 dollars; each tic to the right of the saw tooth represents $100,000 in 1988 dollars. The graph to the left of the saw tooth is a third order polynomial and is identical to the SCF portion of Figure 6.8; the graph to the right of the saw tooth is exponential. Both graphs are based on "best fit" criteria and were fit on the basis of least-squares estimation within the range portrayed.

Sources: Social Welfare Research Institute at Boston College analysis of combined 1989 and 1991 data from Independent Sector's *Survey of Giving and Volunteering in the United States* and 1988 data from the Federal Reserve's *Survey of Consumer Finances*

Amount contributed. For the population of all households, the average amount contributed increases as household net worth increases (from an average contribution of $151 for households that have zero or negative net worth to $238,426 for households that have a net worth of $50 million or more).

Percentage of income contributed. The average percentage of income contributed consistently increases as household net worth increases (from an average of 0.5 percent for households that have zero or negative net worth to 17.8 percent for households that have a net worth of $50 million or more). The upward sloping curve in Figure 6.10 reflects the strong positive relationship between net worth and percentage of income contributed at the very upper reaches of the net worth distribution.

For the subset of households that make a contribution, the relationship between income and percentage of income contributed resembles a "J." Contributing households with negative net worth give about 8.2 percent of their income while households with a net worth of $15,000 to $25,000 contribute only 3.9 percent of their income. However, for households with a net worth of $50 million or more we find contributions reaching 17.8 percent of income.

Participation rate. The rate of participation in charitable giving increases dramatically as net worth increases (from 6.5 percent participation for households that have zero or negative net worth to 100 percent for those that have a net worth of $50 million or more).

Thus it is clear that wealth is strongly related to giving behavior in terms of participation in philanthropy, amounts contributed, and rates of participation. All three measures increase as wealth goes up, just as they increased with income. However, the relationship between percentage of income given and level of income differs from the relationship between percentage of income given and level of wealth. The average percentage of income contributed is roughly constant for households with incomes under $100,000 and increases with income only for households with income above $100,000. In contrast, the average percentage of income contributed increases as net worth increases throughout the positive range of net worth, although the increase is most dramatic among households with net worth in excess of $1,000,000.

Table 6.3. Selected Measures of Contribution by Household Net Worth

Panel	Negative or $0	$1– $5,000	$5,001– $25,000	$25,001– $50,000	$50,001– $100,000	$100,001– $150,000	$150,001– $250,000	$250,001– $500,000	$500,001– $1,000,000	$1,000,001– $10,000,000	$10,000,001– $50,000,000	$50,000,001 or More	Total
1. Sample Size	217	271	335	264	373	253	278	313	193	484	138	24	3143
2. Average Contribution per Household (dollars)	151	77	158	359	386	601	938	1,322	1,821	7,784	41,379	238,426	715
3. Average Percentage of Household Income Contributed	0.5	0.6	0.6	1.3	1.4	1.7	2.2	2.8	2.8	5.5	6.8	17.8	1.5
4. Percentage of Households Participating in Philanthropy	6.5	9.5	14.0	27.2	29.3	42.9	47.2	64.7	75.5	83.6	98.4	100.0	30.7
5. Sample Size, Contributing Households Only	18	22	52	65	120	114	147	210	152	449	133	24	1506
6. Average Contribution per Household, Contributing Households Only (dollars)	2,311	812	1,127	1,319	1,319	1,399	1,986	2,043	2,412	9,305	42,044	238,426	2,330
7. Average Percentage of Household Income Contributed, Contributing Households Only	8.2	5.9	4.4	4.6	4.7	4.1	4.6	4.4	3.7	6.6	6.9	17.8	4.7

Note: Only annual household contributions of $500 or more are recorded in the *Survey of Consumer Finances*. Only contributions of $500 or more are included in this table. The table thus underestimates total and average contributions, as well as contributions as a percentage of income.

The table excludes all cases in which the amount contributed, the participation rate, the percentage of income contributed, or net worth is coded as missing data. Net worth is the sum of the household's assets at current market value less the sum of its liabilities in current dollar terms. No data were collected for the value of furnishings and personal belongings, other than luxury items such as jewelry. The net worth does not take them into account.

All dollar figures refer to 1988 dollars and have not been adjusted for inflation.

Source: Social Welfare Research Institute at Boston College analysis of 1988 data from the Federal Reserve's *Survey of Consumer Finances*

Figure 6.10. Percentage of Household Income Contributed, by Household Net Worth for All Households in the 1989 *Survey of Consumer Finances*

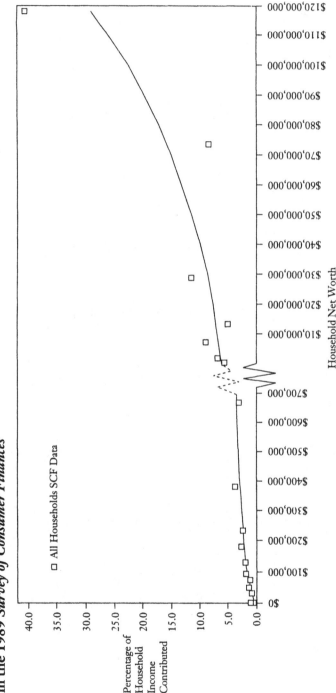

Household Net Worth

Note: The *Survey of Consumer Finances* records contributions of $500 or more annually. On the horizontal axis, each tic to the left of the saw tooth represents $50,000 in 1988 dollars; each tic to the right of the saw tooth represents $5,000,000. The graph to the left of the saw tooth is a power function; the graph to the right of the saw tooth is exponential. Both graphs are based on "best fit" criteria and were fit on the basis of least-squares estimation within the range portrayed.

Sources: Social Welfare Research Institute at Boston College analysis of combined 1989 and 1991 data from Independent Sector's *Survey of Giving and Volunteering in the United States* and 1988 data from the Federal Reserve's *Survey of Consumer Finances*

Additional findings and research directions

We are currently involved in several other research efforts that are related to the content of this chapter. Although these efforts have not yet been completed, we are able to report some preliminary findings.

Charitable giving by low-income households

Preliminary analysis suggests that low-income households contain a large subgroup of persons who are over age 60 and retired. This subgroup further subdivides into a surprisingly sizeable fraction of people who are fairly wealthy—as measured by their net worth—and another fraction, as expected, made up of those who are quite poor. (It should be noted that in the following paragraphs, when we use the term *wealthy* we are referring to net worth.) The wealthy subgroup accounts for a moderately large number of the households with little or no income who make charitable contributions. We are currently exploring the giving behavior of these subgroups to assess the extent to which the higher percentage of income contributed by low-income households is the result of the contributions of these wealthy but low-income households who are apparently contributing to philanthropy from their accumulated wealth rather than from their incomes. Such contributions mathematically would raise the average percentage of income contributed by the low-income group. If this turns out to be the case, the implication is that the high giving by low-income households found in the survey data is not evidence of a very generous low-income poor but of a somewhat generous low-income wealthy.

Variation among very high income households

As presented previously in this chapter, our analysis indicates that households with very high incomes contribute proportionately and progressively more than do other households. Moreover, wealthy households also contribute proportionately more of their income than do both poor households and households of average wealth. But these averages tend to obscure what may be an important underlying phenomenon: a preliminary analysis of the very high income over-sample of the *Survey of Consumer Finances* reveals that a subgroup of these households made large contributions in 1988 while the remainder made modest contributions. This finding is consistent with three different underlying patterns: (1) there are two types of very high income households—one very generous and the other less generous; (2) one type of very high income household makes very large contributions once every few years and modest contributions the rest of the time; or (3) there is some combination of (1) and (2).

To explore this issue further we are attempting to acquire or assemble panel data for very high income households from the *Survey of Consumer Finances* for each of their survey years. An understanding of the underlying pattern is important for fundraisers who would like to know if most wealthy make very large contributions at one time or another and need only to be induced to do so more frequently or if most wealthy seldom make such large contributions and need to be introduced to the notion of substantial giving for the first time.

Up to this point we have investigated charitable giving in terms of participation rate, amount contributed, and percentage of income contributed. However, we have not presented results on the percentage of net worth contributed. We have started to address this issue by examining several correlates of the percentage of net worth contributed. We find that neither level of household income nor level of household wealth is statistically relevant to the percentage of net worth contributed by a household.

There are three possible explanations for this lack of relationship. First, the percentage of net worth may not be a good measure of giving behavior; we are not yet convinced one way or the other. Perhaps there is reason to believe that households with the same level of net worth may perceive their ability to give in entirely different lights. Second, the relationship between percentage of net worth contributed and net worth may be nonlinear and complex. Different underlying patterns of giving may be occurring at different levels of household wealth. Simple correlation analysis is not sufficiently sophisticated to reveal this kind of more complex relationship. Third, the generosity of households as measured by the percentage of their net worth contributed may depend on factors other than household wealth. For example, it may depend more on age, family status, types of assets making up one's net worth, and so forth.

Joint effect of income and wealth

We have found that level of household income and household wealth each separately affect participation rates, amount given, and percentage of income given. Looking at the joint effects of income and wealth we find that, for the most part, the rate of participation, the amount given, and the percentage of income given all increase for each level of income within each level of wealth and for each level of wealth within each level of income. That is, the effects of income and wealth on giving are cumulative. Although the joint effect of income and wealth is positive, wealth tends to make a greater impact than income on amount given and percentage of income given. In contrast, income tends to make a greater impact than wealth on participation rates. We tentatively conclude that, while wealth and income are separately and jointly important for explaining generosity, overall wealth is more important than income, especially when wealth increases to very high levels.

Conclusion

The findings discussed in the foregoing paragraphs are significant for a number of reasons. By analyzing charitable giving across the entire financial spectrum, we are able to correct a long-standing misconception about income and generosity. We can offer the first systematic, albeit preliminary, look at charitable giving by the wealthy. This detailed research suggests several practical implications for fundraising.

Correcting a long-standing misconception

One important empirical contribution of the analysis presented in this chapter is to correct the factual misconception that lower-income households are markedly more generous than upper-income households. In terms of absolute amounts contributed, it is clear that the upper-income groups contribute the lion's share of charitable contributions. More importantly, because lower-income households are substantially less likely to make charitable contributions, it turns out that in the income range up to $100,000 there is a relative equality of generosity measured by percentage of income contributed. Moreover, when we examine patterns of giving for households with income above $100,000, there is a dramatic increase in percentage of income contributed. Thus the popular notion of the generous poor and the stingy rich is simply incorrect.

In fact, lower-income and upper-income households are equally generous, while very high income households are markedly more generous. This should not be taken as an effort to replace the misdirected attack on the rich with adulation. That those with substantially greater discretionary income contribute a larger share than those who may in fact need assistance is neither surprising nor cause for celebration. It is, however, an important fact of philanthropy, the implications of which we address in the next paragraph.

Wealth and philanthropy

The second set of important empirical findings concern the giving patterns of the truly wealthy. Much previous research has spoken about the giving patterns of rich and poor. But that research actually was based on data about income rather than net worth. The *Survey of Consumer Finances* has enabled us not only to extend the analysis to the highest income brackets but to provide—to our knowledge—the first systematic findings on *wealth* and philanthropy. We can now say unequivocally that virtually all the rich are contributors, that they donate very large amounts to charity, and that they give greater proportions of their income to charity than do the poor or the merely affluent. Whether this pattern represents generosity is not for us to say. However, it certainly contradicts the statistical portrait maintained by those who refer to the wealthy as "ungenerous" and "stingy" (see Nielsen, 1992).

Implications for fundraising

Although these findings are quite new and a rich research agenda still awaits our attention, what we have already learned suggests several practical implications for fundraising. Because our findings about upper-income and wealthy households break the most new ground, we focus on the implications in regard to these groups.

First, fundraisers do not need to induce the financially well-off to become givers or create every generous giver de novo. Nearly all upper-income and wealthy households are already participating in charitable giving and many from each group are substantial givers. Second, much of the groundwork for fundraisers has already been done. Unlike lost drivers in Boston who are told "You can't get there from here," fundraisers have it in their capacity to find the way to their goal. Of course, it is their hope and responsibility to attract new donors and elicit the largest possible gifts. But fundraisers generally do not need to turn the wealthy into givers. Usually, that has already occurred.

Thus, fundraisers should attend to getting wealthy donors to do *more* of what they are already doing. That is, in addition to inducing donors to make either an initial or a more frequent large contribution, fundraisers should concentrate on getting donors to focus more on the fundraisers' organization. In a word, fundraisers should abandon the tired and potentially paralyzing imagery of always needing to beckon an unheeding, ungenerous, and uninitiated wealthy population. All are already givers, most are substantial givers, and many have an associate, if not a friend, who is generous.

We recommend three practical tasks, each of which is within the reach of fundraisers. The first is to provide a reason for people who are already givers to focus on a particular cause. Rephrasing Tip O'Neill's dictum about politics, it is also true that all giving is local in the sense that giving reflects the connection between an organization's mission and a funder's moral purpose. Because most individuals at the upper ends of income and wealth are already engaged in charity at some significant level, it is their dedication and not just their generosity that must be secured. The second fundraising task is to engage the very generous givers as fundraising associates. Fundraisers need to learn how to draw on the commitment, access, and contacts of current donors in order to persuade others to make an initial large gift or to increase the frequency and size of their gifts. The third task is to expand the number of such fundraising associates and encourage them to enlarge their own commitments.

And the bottom line? There is a substantial amount of income and wealth available for charitable purposes. Only a few of the wealthy are stingy, many are generous, and all are already active donors at some level. To attract the greater donations, fundraisers need to induce dedication and expanded commitment but not initial generosity.

References

Hodgkinson, V. A., and Weitzman, M. S. *Giving and Volunteering in the United States: Findings from a National Survey, 1990 Edition.* Washington, D.C.: Independent Sector, 1990.

Hodgkinson, V. A., Weitzman, M. S., Noga, S. M., and Gorski, H. A. *Giving and Volunteering in the United States: Findings from a National Survey, 1992 Edition.* Washington, D.C.: Independent Sector, 1992.

Nielsen, W. A. "A Reason to Have Fund Raisers: Our Stingy Rich People." *Chronicle of Philanthropy,* Oct. 6, 1992, pp. 41, 42.

Schervish, P. G., and Havens, J. J. "Do the Poor Pay More? Is the U-Shaped Curve Correct?" Working paper. Chestnut Hill, Mass.: Social Welfare Research Institute, Boston College. 1992.

Schervish, P. G., and Havens, J. J. "Do the Poor Pay More? Is the U-Shaped Curve Correct?" *Nonprofit and Voluntary Sector Quarterly,* 1995, *24* (1), 79–90.

Schervish, P. G., Benz, O., Dulany, P., Murphy, T. B., and Salett, S. *Taking Giving Seriously.* Indianapolis: Indiana University Center on Philanthropy, 1993.

U.S. Bureau of the Census. *Statistical Abstract of the United States, 1993.* 113th Edition. Washington, D.C.: U.S. Government Printing Office, 1993.

PAUL G. SCHERVISH *is associate professor of sociology and director of the Social Welfare Research Institute at Boston College. He directed the Study on Wealth and Philanthropy, an examination of the strategies of living and giving among 130 millionaires.*

JOHN J. HAVENS *is associate director of the Social Welfare Institute and specializes in microsimulation analysis and studies on charitable giving.*

The authors apply their research on the motivations for volunteering to motivations for giving. They identify six personal and social motives that underlie giving decisions. These motives—or functions—can help fundraisers understand different individual and cultural motivations for giving.

Motivations for volunteering and giving: A functional approach

E. Gil Clary, Mark Snyder

THE CHAPTERS in this and the preceding issue of *New Directions for Philanthropic Fundraising* have considered differences that exist in charitable giving: differences between regions of the United States, between ethnic and racial groups, between religious groups, even between men and women. Individuals clearly belong to several cultures of giving. These differences serve as the broader context within which individuals make their own decisions about giving. Although specific cultures affect an individual's charitable donations, also in operation are the psychological processes within individuals. One especially important psychological process concerns the motivational dynamics underlying the charitable gifts of individuals. This chapter addresses the question, "Why do people give in various ways and in various amounts?"

Our work has been devoted to understanding the motivations underlying people's involvement in volunteer work (Clary and Snyder, 1991; Clary, Snyder, and Ridge, 1992). We believe that the

NEW DIRECTIONS FOR PHILANTHROPIC FUNDRAISING, NO. 8, SUMMER 1995 © JOSSEY-BASS PUBLISHERS

insights gained from this study have some clear implications for the study of the motivations of donors. The giving of time and the giving of money, after all, are both variants of a prosocial activity and the two behaviors are correlated with each other. Findings from one area may fruitfully inform the other. The connection itself also raises many important questions, answers to which should enhance our understanding of both forms of giving.

We begin the chapter by describing our work on the motivations of volunteers and providing both the conceptual understandings we have gained and some of the practical applications. We then discuss the ways in which our approach can usefully be applied to questions about charitable giving behavior. Finally, we consider some of the conceptual and practical implications of adopting this strategy. We believe that considering volunteering and giving in this way provides an opportunity to enrich and enhance our understanding of philanthropy in particular and of prosocial behavior in general.

The functional approach to volunteerism

Our approach to the motivations of volunteers is "functional," that is, it is explicitly concerned with the reasons and purposes underlying beliefs and behaviors (Katz, 1960; Smith, Bruner, and White, 1956). We began by asking about the personal and social needs, goals, plans, and motives of the individual that were being fulfilled through volunteer activity. People are purposeful, striving beings; human actions are intended to achieve some goal. Involvement in volunteer activity is similarly purposeful and goal-oriented.

This perspective on behavior is a multimotivational one. Different individuals engaged in the same volunteer activity may well be attempting to satisfy different motivations. Different individuals with different motivations may be alike in that they are involved in the same type of volunteer work but they may turn to different tasks in order to satisfy their own motivations. And any one individual participating in a volunteer activity may well be seeking to satisfy two or more motivations through that one activity.

In our analysis of the psychological functions served by volunteer work we have identified six primary ones. These psychological functions are consistent with previous research on the motivations of volunteers (Clary and Snyder, 1991):

Values function. An individual engages in a volunteer activity to express and act on values important to the self (for example, humanitarian values, values related to serving the community).

Social function. Volunteering helps individuals to fit in and get along with social groups that are important to them.

Career function. Individuals gain career-related experiences by engaging in volunteer work.

Protective function. Individuals engage in volunteer work to cope with anxieties and conflicts and thereby gain some protection for the ego (for example, they reduce guilt or combat feelings of inferiority).

Enhancement function. Volunteer work allows the individual to engage in psychological development and gain in esteem.

Understanding function. Volunteer work is seen to provide opportunities to learn and gain knowledge about the world and to practice skills that would otherwise go unpracticed.

This work on the motivations of volunteers has led to the creation of the Volunteer Functions Inventory (VFI). Each function is measured by five items and completion of the inventory provides a profile of an individual's motivations. Research has provided evidence for the psychometric properties of the VFI as well as support for the multimotivational nature of the psychological foundations of volunteer activity (Ridge and others, 1990).

The functional approach advances a strategy for persuasion. If people have different motivations, communication is most effective if the message speaks to the motivations important to them. Clary and others (1994) found that subjects who received an advertisement that portrayed volunteer work as satisfying a motivation that was important to them had greater intentions to volunteer than did those who received a message that portrayed volunteering as satisfying a motive unimportant to them. Thus, the functional strategy for persuasion stresses the need to tailor communication to the individual.

In sum, the VFI can identify the motivational concerns of current and potential volunteers. Knowledge of the motivations of individuals can then be applied to the recruitment of new volunteers, placement of those new recruits, and then retention of those volunteers (Clary, Snyder, and Ridge, 1992).

We believe that the same functional approach can be used to understand the motivations underlying charitable giving. In this way, we can increase our understanding of this behavior and then utilize the information we gain in the service of the causes pursued by charitable organizations. The key is to show an individual how contributing money to a philanthropic cause can serve his or her personal needs and goals.

The functional approach to understanding charitable giving

The functional approach to understanding charitable donations begins by focusing on the goals of the donor. What purposes are served by giving money? Multiple motivations are likely. In some cases a comparable gift to the same cause may satisfy different motives for different individuals. In other cases different motives will lead people to gravitate toward different charitable causes. Moreover, any one donor may be attempting to fulfill more than one psychological motivation through one donation.

The specific motives identified by the functional approach to volunteer work may also be found in charitable behavior. These functions may overlap with the research findings on wealthy donors, but we believe that the functional framework is applicable to a wide range of donors. The following list is offered as a starting point; we do not wish to imply that our list of functions is exhaustive. As we discuss each function, we will draw on research that suggests that it occurs in decisions about charitable giving. Especially useful is the Independent Sector's (1992) national survey of giving and volunteering in the United States.

Values function

Charitable giving is viewed as an opportunity to express and act on values that are central to the individual. These values are often framed in terms of altruism, humanitarian concern, social responsibility, and community contribution. Research has found that values figure prominently in many varieties of helping, including monetary donations (Amato, Ho, and Partridge, 1984). From Independent Sector's survey, we find that the greater the level of agreement with "I feel a moral duty to help people who suffer," the greater the likelihood that the respondent is a donor. Finally, we might expect that the observed relationship between membership in religious organizations and charitable giving is the result, at least in part, of moral values associated with religion and the obligation felt by individuals to put these values into practice.

Social function

A charitable gift may be a response to social pressure, whether real or imagined, strong or weak. People close to an individual may urge him or her to donate. Or the group to which he or she belongs may have a norm about giving. Independent Sector found that the top two reasons for charitable giving were "being asked to give by someone you know well" and "being asked by the clergy to give." The social function may be partly reflected in social psychological research that has found that giving can be increased through exposure to a charitable model (for example, Bryan and Test, 1967); the example of a donor may exert pressures toward donating on the part of friends and associates.

Career function

This function draws on utilitarian concerns, that is, concern for increasing rewards in the external environment. This function centers on the ways in which a donation may benefit an individual's financial status and material well-being by offering tax advantages as well as career-related benefits. Perhaps a company expects and encourages employees to donate money or perhaps donations to some causes provide contacts that are useful to one's career. In the Independent Sector survey, 42 percent of respondents indicated that tax advantages were a major or minor motivation in their charitable giving or volunteering and 43 percent indicated that being encouraged by an employer was.

Protective function

For some individuals, charitable donations may serve to combat negative feelings. They may donate as a way to reduce feelings of guilt (for example, guilt that they have so much while others have so little). Or they may give now in the hopes that this will cause them to deserve good things in the future. This idea is suggested by the Independent Sector: more than one-third of the respondents to the 1992 survey reported that they felt they were not giving as much as they should to religious organizations, thus hinting at the psychological conflict thought to be at the heart of the protective function. Protective processes in giving are also suggested by the results of an experiment by Cunningham, Steinberg, and Grev (1980). Subjects in whom the feeling of guilt was induced were more likely to contribute money but only if the request was individualized; for example, they were likely to donate to a children's fund if the request was followed by "you owe it to the children."

Enhancement function

Charitable donations may serve to enhance or maintain feelings of self-worth and self-esteem, and more generally, to increase positive mood states. From the Independent Sector survey we learn that 81 percent of the sample indicated that "gaining a sense of personal satisfaction" was a major or minor motivation in their charitable giving or volunteering (p. 224). Moreover, a considerable body of research indicates that helping generally can be increased by creating a positive mood state in the potential helper (see Carlson, Charlin, and Miller, 1988, for a review). In the Cunningham, Steinberg, and Grev experiment mentioned in the previous paragraph, individuals induced to experience a positive mood were also more likely to contribute but only when the inducement followed a positive request (they were asked to give to a children's fund "to help keep the children smiling").

Understanding function

On the face of it, the understanding function that motivates volunteerism may be less transferable than the others to charitable giving. Yet making a donation may allow some individuals to gain some additional understanding about the world. They may learn about a cause through giving to it.

At the heart of this function is the ability to achieve a kind of cognitive growth and development. Thus, it may be operating in those cases where individuals seek to enhance the cultural and intellectual life of their community through a donation. The Independent Sector survey found that 76 percent of respondents reported that "improving the cultural life of the community" was a major or minor goal that they hoped to accomplish through both charitable giving and volunteering.

Summary

The functional perspective offers an organizing framework for conceptions and research on the motivations underlying charitable giving. Furthermore, research related to the motivations of givers appears to be consistent with the psychological functions derived from the functional perspective. We see similarities with the motivational categories that have emerged from recent research on the philanthropy of the wealthy (Prince and File, 1994; Schervish, 1992). At the same time, however, we must remember that empirical support for this perspective on giving is, at best, only suggestive. There is a need to conduct research to verify if donors are attempting to satisfy important personal and social goals and whether these goals conform to the psychological functions we have identified.

To that end, we are currently adapting the VFI for the assessment of the motivations underlying charitable giving. The items of that measure, the Donor Functions Inventory, are presented in Exhibit 7.1. The items are designed to reflect the conceptualization of each function as it applies to charitable giving. The similarity to the functions of the Volunteer Functions Inventory is most apparent in the Values, Social, Enhancement, and Protective functions and less so with the Career and Understanding functions. With this instrument, we can begin to explore the relationships between motivations and actual decisions about giving. Ultimately, we hope to be able to determine the motivational profiles of various "cultures of givers."

Implications of the functional approach

This perspective offers an organizing framework for understanding the motivational dynamics underlying charitable giving and, in doing so, conceptually connects giving and volunteering. The functional perspective may also help us understand the motivational mediators of relationships between demographic variables and charitable giving. Finally, the functional approach suggests strategies for motivating potential givers to give. In the following discussion, we will also see that when we adopt the functional perspective several specific questions that require empirical attention are raised.

Motivational dynamics of giving

First and foremost, the functional approach insists that we understand the psychological goals that individuals pursue through their charitable gifts. The application of the functional approach to volunteerism generally (Ridge and others, 1990; Clary and others, 1994) and to AIDS volunteerism more specifically (Omoto and Snyder, 1995) shows the promise of focusing on the individual's goals. There are important similarities in this perspective and that of Schervish (1992) in his work on the philanthropy of the wealthy,

Exhibit 7.1. Donor Functions Inventory

Values Scale

It is important to help others.

Through giving, I can do something for a cause that is important to me.

Through giving, I can express my concern for those less fortunate than myself.

Giving provides the opportunity to act on my values.

Social Scale

People I am close to place a high value on charitable giving.

People I am close to encourage me to donate.

My family and friends expect me to give.

People I am close to approve of my charitable giving.

Career Scale

Charitable donations are tax deductable.

Involvement in charitable donations allows me to make new contacts that might help my business career.

Charitable giving is good for my career.

My employer expects me to be involved in charitable giving.

Protective Scale

Charitable giving relieves me of some of my guilt about being more fortunate than others.

No matter how bad I've been feeling, giving to others helps me forget about my troubles.

I believe that I owe it to others to donate.

If I give to the less fortunate now, I will deserve good things in the future.

Enhancement Scale

Giving makes me feel important.

Giving increases my self-esteem.

I feel better about myself when I am involved in charitable giving.

Giving puts me in a good mood.

Understanding Scale

Giving allows me to gain a new perspective on things.

I can learn more about the cause to which I am giving.

I want to improve the cultural life of my community.

I want to increase the cultural experiences available to people in my community.

Note: Respondents are instructed: "Please indicate, using the 7-point scale shown below, how important or accurate each of these reasons is for you in making charitable donations." A 7-point response scale then follows: number 1 is anchored by "not at all important/accurate for you" and number 7 by "extremely important/accurate for you."

which emphasizes the strategies the wealthy use in carrying out their charitable behavior. Both approaches seek to uncover the personal goals and purposes for giving.

A focus on the motivational foundations of behavior offers a unifying conceptual framework for charitable behavior and volunteer behavior, inviting us to consider the connections between these two forms of prosocial activity. Clearly, giving and volunteering are related (for example, Ferris and Woolley, 1991; Independent Sector, 1992). However, this point raises important questions, including, "Why does this relationship exist?" and "What are its implications for stimulating each behavior?" The functional approach suggests ways to address these questions.

For example, one might compare the functions pursued by volunteer-givers with those of volunteers (nongivers) and those of givers (nonvolunteers). In what ways are these three classes of "prosocial actors" different? Do volunteer-givers have more intense motivations compared with the other two groups? Do volunteer-givers have a wider range of motivations, some satisfied through volunteering and some through giving? Is it more desirable to be a volunteer-giver or to "specialize" in volunteering or giving? Do volunteering and giving together result in increased satisfaction and commitment or lead instead to burnout? Answers to these questions will not only enhance our understanding of the motivational dynamics underlying prosocial behavior but also offer important practical applications.

Motivational mediators

Given that different groups or cultures exhibit differences in giving, are there motivational processes that contribute to group differences? For example, Independent Sector's 1992 national survey reports that (in terms of percentage of givers within the sample) females are more likely to contribute than males, older people more likely than younger people, and people with education beyond high school more likely than those with a high school degree or less.

The functional perspective provides a systematic way to think about the motivational processes that underlie these differences. Indeed, the Donor Functions Inventory offers a method for actually assessing those differences. As a first step, it can be used to determine the functional profiles of different demographic groups. Then, for each specific group or culture, it can be used to discover which motivations were extremely important, moderately important, and relatively unimportant.

Promoting charitable donations

There are considerable practical advantages to be gained from uncovering motivations. However, the functional approach not only provides a framework for understanding behavior but also offers a strategy for persuasion. Messages designed to promote behavior should tailor appeals to the motivations of the recipients, demonstrating to individuals how psychological functions important to them can be served through the suggested actions. The efficacy of this approach to persuasion has been demonstrated recently in the realm of volunteerism (Clary and others, 1994).

Appeals for donations to charitable causes should show the message receiver that giving will serve his or her personal and social goals. If we know that values-related concerns are salient to a potential donor or group of potential donors (as determined by the motivational profile of the recipient's demographic group assessed with the DFI), an appeal requesting a donation would stress the way in which it will enable expression of these values. But a message targeted at an individual for whom enhancement motivations are central would stress the good feelings that come from making a charitable donation.

This approach to persuasion is not limited to advertisements. It applies to a broad range of attempts to influence, including face-to-face interactions with potential donors. The functional approach encourages fundraisers to attempt to understand the needs and goals of potential givers and then present the ways in which a donation will help them achieve these goals. In other words, fundraisers must speak the motivational language of the potential donor.

Conclusion

The functional approach offers a framework in which to think about charitable giving and its motivational foundations, the relationship between giving and volunteering, and the psychological links that may exist between demographic characteristics and giving. The connection between them all is the way in which these behaviors serve psychological goals and needs. Moreover, the functional approach is highly practical as it suggests ways to promote prosocial activities. It is critical to match motivations that are important to the donor with the opportunity for a donation.

We believe that the functional perspective creates a "win-win-win" situation. The organization or cause stands to receive funds that are necessary for it to accomplish its tasks. The donor satisfies personal goals that are important to him or her. And researchers gain some insight into an intriguing and socially important behavior.

References

Amato, P., Ho, R., and Partridge, S. "Responsibility Attribution and Helping Behavior in the Ash Wednesday Bushfires." *Australian Journal of Psychology*, 1984, *36*, 191–203.

Bryan, J. H., and Test, M. A. "Models and Helping: Naturalistic Studies in Aiding Behavior." *Journal of Personality and Social Psychology*, 1967, *6*, 400–407.

Carlson, M., Charlin, V., and Miller, N. "Positive Mood and Helping Behavior: A Test of Six Hypotheses." *Journal of Personality and Social Psychology*, 1988, *55*, 211–229.

Clary, E. G., and Snyder, M. "A Functional Analysis of Altruism and Prosocial Behavior: The Case of Volunteerism." In M. Clark (ed.), *Review of Personality and Social Psychology: Vol. 12.* Newbury Park, Calif.: Sage, 1991.

Clary, E. G., Snyder, M., and Ridge, R. "Volunteers' Motivations: A Functional Strategy for the Recruitment, Placement, and Retention of Volunteers." *Nonprofit Management and Leadership*, 1992, *2*, 333–350.

Clary, E., Snyder, M., Ridge, R., Meine, P., and Haugen, J. "Matching Messages to Motives in Persuasion: A Functional Approach to Promoting Volunteerism." *Journal of Applied Social Psychology*, 1994, *24*, 1129–1149.

Cunningham, M., Steinberg, J., and Grev, R. "Wanting to and Having to Help: Separate Motivations for Positive Mood and Guilt-Induced Helping." *Journal of Personality and Social Psychology*, 1980, *38*, 181–192.

Ferris, J. M., and Woolley, J. M. "Gifts of Time and Money." Paper presented at the Independent Sector 1991 Spring Research Forum, Cleveland, Ohio, Mar. 1991.

Independent Sector. *Giving and Volunteering in the United States.* Washington, D.C.: Independent Sector, 1992.

Katz, D. "The Functional Approach to the Study of Attitudes." *Public Opinion Quarterly*, 1960, *24*, 163–204.

Omoto, A. M., and Snyder, M. "Sustained Helping Without Obligation: Motivation, Longevity of Service, and Perceived Attitude Change Among AIDS Volunteers." *Journal of Personality and Social Psychology*, 1995, *68*, 671–686.

Prince, R. A., and File, K. M. *The Seven Faces of Philanthropy: A New Approach to Cultivating Major Donors.* San Francisco: Jossey-Bass, 1994.

Ridge, R., Snyder, M., Clary, E., French, S., Meine, P., Pederson, J., and Copeland, J. "The Volunteer Functions Inventory: Toward an Understanding of the Motives to Volunteer." Paper presented at the annual meeting of the American Psychological Association, Boston, June 1990.

Schervish, P. G. "Adoption and Altruism: Those with Whom I Want to Share a Dream." *Nonprofit and Voluntary Sector Quarterly*, 1992, *21*, 327–350.

Smith, M., Bruner, J., and White, R. *Opinions and Personality.* New York: Wiley, 1956.

E. GIL CLARY *is professor of psychology at the College of St. Catherine in St. Paul, Minnesota, and the author of many studies on volunteers and volunteers' motivations.*

MARK SNYDER *is professor of psychology at the University of Minnesota.*

*Studies on philanthropy are expanding their scope
to encompass many ways of looking at different cultures of giving. One approach is to identify major
donor groups by the motivations, values, and beliefs
they share. One such approach is the Seven Faces
framework, which has been successfully applied in a
number of development situations.*

8

Philanthropic cultures of mind

Russ Alan Prince, Karen Maru File

THE VALUE of identifying subcultures—groups of people who share
values, lifestyles, attitudes, beliefs, or behavior—has been well
established in fields other than philanthropy and fundraising
(Kotler, 1991; Lesser and Hughes, 1986; Johnson, 1986; Leibtag,
1986; Wills, 1985; Wind, 1978; and Plummer, 1974). By identifying the subcultures within the population it interacts with, an institution can more effectively tailor its programs to the values, needs,
and beliefs of the targeted group or groups. In the area of fundraising, a case could be made for grouping major donors within individual subculture of giving and then making an effort to understand
the subcultural membership of individual donors. With this kind of
understanding, strong donor-centered development at the group
level—in addition to the individual level—becomes possible.

The first step in defining such cultures of giving is to explore major
donor motivations, values, and beliefs as already understood in the
field and then to specify groups representing subcultures on the basis

NEW DIRECTIONS FOR PHILANTHROPIC FUNDRAISING, NO. 8, SUMMER 1995 © JOSSEY-BASS PUBLISHERS

of those established motivations. Fortunately, there is a substantial body of research on which such an effort can be founded. A number of studies explore the charitable motivations and practices of donors such as those who contribute to the United Way campaigns (Harvey, 1990; Guy and Patton, 1988; Smith, 1980) and provide thoughtful analyses of trends in philanthropy in the United States (Hodgkinson and Weitzman, 1994; Weisbrod, 1988; Jencks, 1987).

Until recently, despite their relative importance, large-scale research among major donors was limited (Prince, 1992; Magat, 1990). This gap is now being filled. In recent years, the importance to philanthropic activity of such personal motivations as altruism, beliefs, instrumental motives, desire to create a memorial, community connection, and peer pressure have been established (Boris, 1987; Cermak, File, and Prince, 1994). The importance of religious orientation has also been noted (Wuthnow, Hodgkinson, and Associates, 1990), particularly as it interacts with social class and social culture (Odendahl, 1990). Finally, personal values, life experiences, and communication style have been shown to affect philanthropic behavior (Schervish, 1991).

These studies of the values, beliefs, and motivations of donors provided the foundation for the Seven Faces research program.

Methodology

A complete discussion of the data collection and analytical methods used to develop the Seven Faces profiles is provided elsewhere (Prince and File, 1994), so only a brief review is provided here. A detailed questionnaire was developed consisting of statements representing motivations, values, and beliefs drawn from the literature on philanthropy. Then a sample of major donors was constructed. Major donors were defined as individuals with $1 million or more in liquid assets who are philanthropically inclined. Cluster analysis was then used to identify the major subcultures of philanthropy among these wealthy donors; these are the Seven Faces.

Since the initial study, these research results have been repeatedly validated. First, members of each segment have been recontacted and interviewed at length over the telephone in order to ascertain the validity of the classification scheme. In addition, nonprofit resource development managers have confirmed the usefulness of the framework. In the past year, eighteen replications of the framework (involving over three thousand affluent respondents) in different nonprofit domains have been conducted (*Chronicle of Philanthropy*, 1994). These show that the Seven Faces framework is stable across types of nonprofits and that major donors and nonprofits are joined through systems of shared values.

The Seven Faces profiles

The use of the psychographic method described in the previous section culminated in the creation of seven motivation-based groups that are characterized by the primary benefits each seeks when giving to nonprofits. It should be noted that because motivations change over time—all people are affected by life events—the Seven Faces framework should be seen as a way to understand the principal motivations operating at one point in time.

The personality types that the Seven Faces describe are briefly described in the following paragraphs. (For a comprehensive description, see Prince and File, 1994.) The number shown in parentheses is the proportion of all major donors represented by that type.

1. *Communitarians* (26 percent). Communitarians are those who might say, "If I'm going to help someone, it's going to be my neighbors." The core cultural value of Communitarians is to do what they can to improve their local social and economic setting. Thus, they select nonprofits that serve the needs of their community and concentrate their giving on local cultural, religious, and educational institutions.

2. *The Devout* (21 percent). Devotion to religious life constitutes the core cultural value of the Devout. The Devout can be typified by

the following quote, "Thanks to the Almighty, I have the means to improve the lives of others." They obviously support nonprofits for religious and spiritual reasons. In addition, their philanthropy is prompted by the belief that God intends them individually to help others. Unlike Communitarians, the Devout do not restrict their philanthropy to local charitable organizations. National and international causes are supported if they meet their religious criteria.

3. *Investors* (15 percent). Investors share a unique set of beliefs about the role of philanthropy in their lives. Although they enjoy giving, they emphasize financial considerations in all charitable decisions. As one Investor explained, "I want to be smart about the financial aspects of how I give." Because Investors see their contribution as an investment—at least in part—they are far more likely than other major donors to be concerned about the tax and estate consequences and the benefits of giving; they tend to engage in investorlike behavior with respect to nonprofits.

4. *Socialites* (11 percent). Socialites are involved in philanthropy through their personal support systems and cultural groups. As one Socialite explained, "We all work together, my friends and I, to raise money for charity." Socialites often support arts and educational nonprofits as well as religious nonprofits. As would be expected, these individuals are attracted to the social circle that surrounds nonprofits and find the social functions especially appealing.

5. *Repayers* (10 percent). Repayers give out of a sense of obligation and gratitude. Often they have personally benefited at an earlier time from the services of a nonprofit such as a medical or educational institution. A typical Repayer will explain, "I just made a major gift to the hospital that took care of my wife." Repayers concentrate their philanthropy on the institutions that matter to them and are less likely to support a broad range of nonprofits.

6. *Altruists* (9 percent). Altruists support nonprofits because doing so gives their lives a greater sense of purpose; in fact, despite their name, they seek self-fulfillment. The difference between Altruists and the Devout is that the Devout usually identify with a traditional religious faith or institution whereas Altruists are focused on more

personal values. As one Altruist elaborated, "For me, philanthropy is a process of personal development and a way to help others."

7. *Dynasts* (8 percent). Dynasts fulfill the image of the wealthy family with a tradition of philanthropy. Inherited wealth is concentrated in this group. Philanthropic motivations develop through socialization; giving is something the family has always done, a value it stands for. Dynasts believe it is expected of them to support nonprofits.

Understanding the different cultures of philanthropy can help fundraisers be more efficient and effective on behalf of their organizations. An understanding of the values shared by wealthy philanthropists gained through the Seven Faces framework can be helpful to many philanthropic efforts. It can aid in the successful cultivation of new affluent donors through charity network recruiting (Prince and File, 1994). It may also be used to compare and contrast the profiles of major donors across different types of nonprofits (*Chronicle of Philanthropy*, 1994).

In the following section, we consider one example. How could the Seven Faces framework be applied to planned giving and especially to charitable estate planning?

Charitable estate planning

Charitable estate planning is not merely estate planning that uses charitable giving strategies. At its core, charitable estate planning is about philanthropy and doing what is best for the wealthy donor. "Charitable estate planning is the process of redistributing assets to maximize their value enabling the philanthropic affluent to be charitable in ways that work best for them" (Prince, McBride, and File, 1994, p. 38). The charitable estate planning process supports the planned giving strategies and promotions of nonprofits. The process has three major phases: philanthropic personality, situational needs and objectives, and the charitable estate plan.

Philanthropic personality

The behavior of prospective affluent donors is a function of their philanthropic personalities. Although most of the affluent by far are philanthropically inclined, not all are. Philanthropic inclinations are moderated by other aspects of the personality, such as the balance struck between self-interest and altruism, the degree of dependence on a social group for information and decision making, involvement in philanthropy (where involvement is understood as a construct representing degree of importance and signification), and tolerance of risk. All of these aspects of the philanthropic personality are reflected in the Seven Faces schema. By using it as a foundation for charitable estate planning, the focus is always on the charitable orientation of the affluent individual. However, knowledge about and interest in planned giving varies across major donor types. In the case of charitable remainder trusts, for example, almost half of Socialites, the Devout, Repayers, and Communitarians are very interested in learning more about the option. But fewer than one in five Altruists are. In contrast, interest in private foundations is extremely high across the board (Prince and File, 1994).

Understanding the philanthropic personality of the affluent allows an understanding of the charity networks that support individual donors. Charity networks are the systems of social relationships donors rely on to identify, screen, select, and support the nonprofits they become involved with. Socialites are known for enjoying the charity network of friends with whom they exchange charitable commitments. Communitarians rely heavily on charitable networks made up of business associates and members of civic associations. More than 80 percent of each of the Seven Faces types say their charitable network is very important to them. Repayers are the exceptions (Prince and File, 1994). Because Repayers are motivated to support a specific institution as a result of their personal history with it, they do not need a network to support that process.

Addressing the needs of the philanthropic affluent from the perspective of charitable estate planning has a number of implications for nonprofits. For one, they should recognize that knowledge and interest varies widely among major donor types. It is essential to meet donors at their current level of interest and sophistication. The Seven Faces categories offer a useful guide to doing this. In addition, development efforts and materials should focus on networks of major donor prospects by type rather than simply on individuals.

Situational needs and objectives

Affecting affluent potential donors are their situational needs and objectives which, therefore, must be taken into account if planned gifts are to be made. There are three sets of situational needs and objectives; financial, lifestyle, and charitable. It is essential to pay attention to the current financial position of the affluent donor in the same way that it is necessary to understand the nature of the lifestyle that individual has and desires. Finally, although the Seven Faces schema provides insights into motivations, it is still necessary to understand clearly personal charitable agendas as they relate to individual nonprofits. Only by being attentive to these concerns will a nonprofit be able to promote effectively the creation of planned gifts while remaining donor-centered.

At this stage, the Seven Faces schema can help development professionals modify case statements, other positioning materials, and approaches to the type and personal situation of each major donor. For example, a university seeking funds to support a small business incubator might target Communitarians and stress the benefits of such a center to the local economy. When the university targets Repayers, though, the emphasis would be on the personal benefit they would gain in helping others attain the kind of success they have.

To demonstrate to prospective donors that their situation is understood and appreciated, it can be helpful to persuade a current major donor of the same personality profile as the prospective donor to offer a testimonial on the nonprofit's behalf. The current major donor might be able to craft a vision of support for the nonprofit that would be particularly effective in motivating the prospective donor to act. More than three-quarters of major donors agree that having another major donor *like themselves* explain the benefits of nonprofit support is very important to them (Prince and File, 1994).

Several development efforts can help nonprofits understand more clearly the situation of prospective major donors in the context of charitable estate planning:

Profile current major donors by type by using the Seven Faces schema or any other that works best for the particular nonprofit.

Interact sufficiently with prospective major donors in order to keep abreast of changes in their situations.

Create a program where current and prospective major donors of the same type can interact, thereby providing positive reinforcement of the message.

The charitable estate plan

Once a major donor is motivated to provide more than nominal support, the question of strategy within the context of charitable estate planning becomes the central issue. As public policy in the United States has established incentives for philanthropy, major donors can contribute to nonprofits in a variety of ways. Beside direct gifts of cash or property there exist numerous types of planned gifts, including charitable remainder trusts and gift annuities. Each of the Seven Faces groupings varies in type of need. Thus, one of the keys to the success of charitable estate planning is to involve major donors in the construction of the plan itself.

When the donor agrees to provide significant support to a nonprofit, the task is to make the relationship as rewarding as possible for the donor. For almost all major donors, satisfaction with nonprofits grows as their personal participation increases (Cermak, File, and Prince, 1991). However, not all nonprofits are as effective as they might be in getting donors involved in their ongoing operations or in the charitable estate planning process. For example, some major donors feel they are only infrequently provided with the information they need about the nonprofits they are involved with; Repayers, the Devout, Altruists, and Investors are most likely to believe they are uninformed. In addition, some major donors feel their opinions are not asked for frequently enough; Socialites, Repayers, and Altruists are less likely than others to feel that the nonprofits have enlisted their viewpoint sufficiently (Prince and File, 1994).

Empowering the donor by getting him or her personally involved in the charitable estate planning process and ensuring continued active involvement implies that nonprofits undertake a number of actions:

• Using the Seven Faces framework, ensure that areas of major donor interest and commitment are known. Understand especially the nature of the involvement donors seek in the charitable estate planning process.

• Make sure meaningful information about charitable giving opportunities and donor involvement in the areas of interest is communicated to the major donor at the frequency and through the medium they prefer.

Conclusion

The constructs of culture and subculture are useful new paradigms for understanding groups of donors. Looking at giving and givers through the lens of geography, ethnicity, religion, and gender all add to our understanding of philanthropical behavior. Yet the differences and similarities discussed in the other chapters of *New Directions for Philanthropic Fundraising* are only part of the complex story. The Seven Faces framework presented in this chapter represents one more way to understand affluent donors through the motivations, beliefs, and values they bring to philanthropy.

The Seven Faces framework describes the principal motivations of major donor groups. Most nonprofits will find they have a mix of major donor types. Adjusting to the complexity of each organization's donor base can be accomplished. Thus, nonprofits need to address the variety of donor motivations by creating case statements tailored to different donor groups, implementing processes to identify the individual needs of donors in the context of their Seven Faces type, gaining the support of the existing base of donors, and creating mutually beneficial long-term relationships with major donors.

Attention to the donor's complex needs is the hallmark of good fundraising. An understanding of the seven types of major donors—with the help of the Seven Faces profiles—can help us understand their differences and similarities and then focus more effectively on them in our fundraising efforts.

References

Boris, E. "Creation and Growth: A Survey of Private Foundations." In T. Odendahl (ed.), *America's Wealthy and the Future of Foundations.* New York: Foundation Center, 1987.

Cermak, D.S.P., File, K. M., and Prince, R. A. "Complaining and Praising in Nonprofit Exchanges: When Satisfaction Matters Less." *Journal of Consumer Satisfaction, Dissatisfaction, and Complaining Behavior,* 1991, *4,* 180–187.

Cermak, D.S.P., File, K. M., and Prince R. A. "A Benefit Segmentation of the Major Donor Market." *Journal of Business Research,* 1994, *29* (2), 121–130.

Chronicle of Philanthropy. Series of articles on Seven Faces and various nonprofits beginning May 17, 1994.

Guy, B. S., and Patton, W.E. "The Marketing of Altruistic Causes: Understanding Why People Help." *Journal of Services Marketing,* 1988, 2, 5–16.

Harvey, J. W. "Benefit Segmentation for Fund Raisers." *Journal of the Academy of Marketing Science,* 1990, *18,* 77–86.

Hodgkinson, V., and Weitzman, M. *Giving and Volunteering in the United States.* Washington, D.C.: Independent Sector, 1994.

Jencks, C. "Who Gives to What?" In W. W. Powell (ed.), *The Nonprofit Sector: A Research Handbook.* New Haven, Conn.: Yale University Press, 1987.

Johnson, E. M. "Marketing Planning for Nonprofit Organizations." *Nonprofit World,* 1986, *4,* 20–21, 38.

Kotler, P. *Marketing Management.* (7th ed.) New York: Prentice Hall, 1991.

Lesser, J. A., and Hughes, M. A. "The Generalizability of Psychographic Market Segments Across Geographic Location." *Journal of Marketing,* 1986, *50,* 18–27.

Leibtag, B. "Marketing to the Affluent." *Journal of Accountancy,* 1986, *162,* 165–71.

Magat, R. *Prospective Views of Research on Philanthropy and the Voluntary Sector.* New York: Foundation Center, 1990.

Odendahl, T. *Charity Begins at Home: Generosity and Self-Interest Among the Philanthropic Elite.* New York: Basic Books, 1990.

Plummer, J. T. "The Concept and Application of Life Style Segmentation." *Journal of Marketing,* 1974, *38,* 33–37.

Prince, R. A. "Charitable Trusts: The Magic Bullet." *Trusts & Estates,* 1992, *131,* 45–54.

Prince, R. A., and File, K. M. *The Seven Faces of Philanthropy: A New Approach to Cultivating Major Donors.* San Francisco: Jossey-Bass, 1994.

Prince, R. A., McBride, W., and File, K. M. *The Charitable Estate Planning Process: How to Find and Work with the Philanthropic Affluent.* Lexington, Ky.: Lexington House, 1994.

Schervish, P. G. "Philanthropy Among the Wealthy: Empowerment, Motivation, and Strategy." Paper presented to the Rocky Mountain Philanthropic Institute, Vail, Colo., July 22, 1991.

Smith, S. M. "Giving to Charitable Organizations : A Behavioral Review and Framework for Increasing Commitment." In J. C. Olson (ed.), *Advances in Consumer Research,* 7. Ann Arbor, Mich.: Association for Consumer Research, 1980.

Weisbrod, B. A. *The Nonprofit Economy.* Cambridge, Mass.: Harvard University Press, 1988.

Wills, G. "Dividing and Conquering: Strategies for Segmentation." *International Journal of Bank Marketing,* 1985, *3,* 36–46.

Wind, Y. "Issues and Advances in Segmentation Research." *Journal of Market Research,* 1978, *15,* 317–337.

Wuthnow, R., Hodgkinson, V. A., and Associates. *Faith and Philanthropy in America.* San Francisco: Jossey-Bass, 1990.

RUSS ALAN PRINCE *is president of Prince and Associates of Stratford, Connecticut, and coauthor of* The Seven Faces of Philanthropy: A New Approach to Cultivating Major Donors.

KAREN MARU FILE *is associate professor of marketing in the Graduate School of Business at the University of Connecticut. She is coauthor of* The Seven Faces of Philanthropy: A New Approach to Cultivating Major Donors.

We often talk in the vernacular about differences between generations, but we rarely apply the idea to our philanthropical activities. This chapter introduces a model of generational archetypes that can explain a lot about donor behavior and be an important tool when planning the appropriate fundraising strategy.

9

Philanthropic cultures of generational archetypes

Charles L. Eastman

THE FUNDRAISER analyzes numbers, motivations, styles of giving, and vehicles for giving. The chapters in this and the preceding issue of *New Directions for Philanthropic Fundraising* examine in detail the different cultures of giving thriving in the United States today. But still lacking is what might be called the generational view. This chapter offers a look at how the generational view can help in the fundraising process. The chapter is divided into two parts. The first part informs the reader of a lens through which we may understand more clearly the vast expanse of history, the mechanism that I call the Strauss-Howe model. In the second part, two examples illustrate how the Strauss-Howe model can explain the different leadership styles of different generational cultures and provide a successful multigenerational approach to fundraising.

NEW DIRECTIONS FOR PHILANTHROPIC FUNDRAISING, NO. 8, SUMMER 1995 © JOSSEY-BASS PUBLISHERS

Looking at the ways in which different generations behave is useful for conceptualizing donor motivations. This is true because it is not chronological age alone but membership in a generation that has a profound impact. Cultures of giving all have a generational component. Some appreciation of the generational archetypes, then, can help make fundraising appeals more targeted and focused.

The Strauss-Howe model

How many times we have attended seminars that ask us to give our attention to statistics that demonstrate either great opportunity for us or great donor dissatisfaction with our methods. Certainly, donor recognition is always an important aspect of successful fundraising. But what kind of recognition? What if we could get a larger picture of key characteristics describing each generation? What if we had a model that described the culture of our own moment in history and then compared it to other historical moments?

We have such a model. It is found in the book *Generations: The History of America's Future, 1584 to 2069* (Strauss and Howe, 1991). The Strauss-Howe model was researched and developed through an examination of U.S. history. Fundraisers who work in other countries will need to decide for themselves what application, if any, the model might have for them.

Strauss and Howe began with the observation that four generational archetypes have repeated themselves with regularity throughout U.S. history. These four archetypes are the Idealist, the Reactive, the Civic, and the Adaptive. The four generations alternate in dominant and recessive types. The Idealist is a dominant generation. It often sets the ideological framework for generations to come. The Reactive is a recessive generation. As its name indicates, it reacts—with great individuality and pragmatism—to its role as scapegoat, as the generation blamed for society's ills. The Civic is a dominant generation that wins wars, overcomes social difficulties, builds social institutions, and, more recently, develops technology. The Adaptive is once again a recessive generation. It refines and improves upon the accomplishments of the Civic generation.

According to Strauss and Howe, almost every great cycle of U.S. history has seen the succession of these four generational archetypes repeated. (The exception is the Civil War period, but for the purposes of this chapter it is unnecessary to detain the reader with a discussion.) The four broad historical cycles in the United States that Strauss and Howe understand to be completed are the Colonial Cycle (1588–1692), the Revolutionary Cycle (1693–1789), the Civil War Cycle (1790–1865), and the Great Power Cycle (1866–1945). We are now living through the Millennial Cycle. This cycle is characterized by a Boom Awakening (1967–1980) and a crisis, which will peak around 2016. The Strauss-Howe framework suggests that the large cycles in our history are all characterized by an ideological awakening that is followed by a civic crisis some thirty to fifty years later.

Strauss and Howe invite practitioners of all disciplines to test their model (p. 17). Thus, an examination of the roles of the generational archetypes can help philanthropical organizations determine where a fundraising philosophy should direct them for the future.

Generational archetypes today

First, it is necessary to describe briefly the generations that are alive today; these generations either will or are giving to our organizations. (I hasten to add that these generational archetypes—or types as Strauss and Howe call them—are demographic cohorts delineated not simply from historical events but also from population, economic, and social data.) Next, we will look at how generational archetypes are affecting the organizations we serve and then search for successful models for intergenerational approaches to giving.

The six generational cohorts alive today can be divided among the four archetypal generations. In the following paragraphs I describe these generational cohorts, giving the years of their birth, the archetypal generation they belong to, some of their demographic characteristics, and the possible implications for fundraising considerations.

The Lost Generation. Born between 1883 and 1900, this generation is of the Reactive type. Members of the Lost Generation are dying today. They are leaving their now-modest estates to the institutions or groups that accepted them as "members of the family" without quashing their individuality or independence, institutions such as churches and schools. They also leave gifts for the advancement of the profession that nurtured them economically. Some, like Dr. Norman Vincent Peale, leave considerable estates to private foundations—in Dr. Peale's case, to one that perpetuates his sermons and writings.

A common mistake of older fundraisers—who like this author can remember missionary grandparents—is to approach members of the Lost Generation as if they are dour old Idealists. Whether they have enormous wealth or very little wealth, the nearly one million living members of this generation will consider annual giving and planned giving, as one once remarked, as doing "something practical" for single-parent families or, as another remarked, as a way to "raise the flag" when she or a family member experienced a personal victory.

The GI Generation. Born between 1901 and 1924, this generation displays the dominant characteristics of the Civic type. Strauss and Howe characterize this generation as the most collectivistic ever in the history of the United States (pp. 261–278). But then one does not beat the Great Depression, win a war, discover a cure for polio, invent the computer, and develop the Social Security system without some collaborative effort! As with most Civic generation types, this one divides the roles of the sexes more clearly than other generations. GI men will continue to give in large amounts, both collectively and individually—this generation does have the money. GI women, who are accustomed to some male guidance, tend not to be as secure in their gift commitments.

Nearly all types of planned giving vehicles may hold interest for both GI men and women. A man of this generation might think in particular about a charitable remainder gift while a woman might consider a gift annuity. The years during which campaigns could have expected to gain enormous annual contributions from this generation are now past. New fundraising strategies must be implemented both for the GIs and for succeeding generations.

The Silent Generation. Born between 1925 and 1942, the Silent Generation is of the Adaptive type. These individuals were born during a time of great need but went on to rocket to enormous wealth. However, the generation suffers from guilt and anxiety, ironically the result of some of its greatest contributions. This generation is left wealthy but without clear meaning and direction.

Some believe that this generation will leave most of its money to grandchildren in order to assuage the guilt it feels for the broken families in which its own children grew up. Planned-giving expert Robert F. Sharpe, Jr., suggested (at a talk at Broward County's Second Planned Giving Seminar, Ft. Lauderdale, Mar. 18, 1994) that gift annuities meet this generation's need to give and ensure security for grandchildren. Because Adaptive generations are traditionally technologically oriented and because this generation is already racked with guilt, a highly technical rather than an emotional approach could get the best results.

The Boomer Generation. Born between 1942 and 1960, this dominant generation is of the Idealist type. As Idealists they have been driven by visions both liberal (in the case of older Boomers) and conservative (in the case of younger Boomers). The immediacy and effortlessness portrayed on television has encouraged them to make quick selections and snap judgments. It has created in them the illusion that direct services are "good" and that overhead and administration costs are "bad." Perhaps an underlying motivation for Boomers is that they do not want to throw "big bucks" at the very GI institutions they grew up distrusting.

The fundraiser must discover constructive ways of engaging Boomers in hands-on experience that gives moral capital to a grand moral movement. The organization Habitat for Humanity and others in the environmental movement in general seem to typify Boomer interests; United Ways, Jewish federations, and big hospitals do not. A recent New York State probate will reveals the values of a Jewish Boomer who died of AIDS: he left a six-figure amount to the United Nations for care of children in the Central American country where he discovered his spirituality. A lesser amount went to an at-home meal delivery service for people with AIDS. Not one dollar went to the Jewish federation, the hospital that cared for him, or close members of his family, as would be expected from a GI will.

Generation X. Born between 1961 and 1981, this generation is, once again, Reactive. According to Strauss and Howe (pp. 317–334), no previous generation has been so marketed to. Many have "McJobs" that pay minimum wages and offer little promise of great wealth. They often come from or are part of dysfunctional families.

As far as fundraising is concerned, this generation will work hard on events. These individuals will give a Saturday or two, help out where needed. They have the time: the future promises them no great commitment so they are unable to commit themselves to their futures. Institutions would do well to develop relationships with members of this generation now. Such relationships can develop into the missing family this group so desperately seeks and needs.

The Millennials. Born beginning in 1982, this generation is once again of the Civic type. Obviously, the statistics are not yet in on it, but we can expect a lot of school and Sunday school collections. These individuals are likely to be as collectivistic in their fundraising perspectives as their GI great-grandparents and grandparents were in the early part of this century.

Case study: Three generations on a board

To understand how each generational culture differs from the others, one need only examine giving activity on one specific board of directors. What follows is a breakdown of giving history by generation for a board of directors of a social welfare, action, and advocacy organization in a large city in the southeastern United States.

Table 9.1 shows that individuals of the GI Generation give an annual average outright gift ($1,512) that is almost three times as much as that given by members of the Silent Generation ($584). The ratio of GIs' to Boomers' average annual gift ($104) is nearly fifteen to one.

Table 9.2 shows outside gifts brought into the organization in the most recent fiscal year by board members who are closely allied with the donating foundations or institutions. The totals shown

Table 9.1. Total Giving over Number of Years and Resultant Average Annual Gift by Generations (dollars)

GI			Silent			Boomer		
Total Gift	No. Years	Average Annual Gift	Total Gift	No. Years	Average Annual Gift	Total Gift	No. Years	Average Annual Gift
613	6	102	75	1	75	0	0	0
26,025	19	1,370	750	1	750	200	1	200
8,452	6	1,409	100	1	100	0	0	0
1,645	8	206	1,050	4	263	1,165	6	194
118,315	18	6,573	0	0	0	0	0	0
12,520	19	659	0	0	0	0	0	0
7,760	15	517	40	1	40	0	0	0
4,685	7	669	6,025	13	463	75	1	75
9,911	5	1,982	32,487	15	2,166	2,830	6	472
19,583	12	1,632	9,595	16	600	710	7	101
			49,504	13	3,808			
			0	0	0			
			1,225	6	204			
			4,800	6	800			
			3,110	10	311			
			1,520	7	217			
			410	3	137			
Total								
209,509	115	15,119	110,691	97	9,934	4,980	21	1,024
Number of Board Members								
10			17			10		
Average								
20,951	12	1,512	6,511	6	584	498	2	104

Table 9.2. Foundation and Institutional Gifts with Average by Generation (dollars)

	GI	Silent	Boomer
	17,500	11,500	5,000
	5,000	300	600
	500	1,000	500
	500	5,000	20,000
	300	600	1,500
		500	500
		22,500	
		5,000	
Total	23,800	46,400	28,100
Number of Board Members	5	8	6
Average	4,760	5,800	4,683
Total Number of Board Members	10	17	10
Average per Total Number of Board Members	2,380	2,729	2,810

demonstrate a preponderance of Silent participation in this kind of giving. Indeed, the Silent Generation is used to making GI money work more productively. The close connections Boomers have—they call it *networking* in characteristic computerese—bring in the second highest total amount. (Amounts were derived from the notion that the board member was a necessary ingredient to accessing the gift, in most cases the most significant ingredient. Amounts were distributed among board members in cases in which two or more worked as a team to bring in one gift; that is, if three people brought in a gift from Foundation A for $9,000, each got credited with $3,000 regardless of their generation.)

When one overlays foundational and institutional gifts obtained indirectly over outright gifts by board members, one discovers that the GI Generation is still able to produce the highest annual average gift ($3,892 or $1,512 outright plus $2,380 institutional or foundational). The Silent is second ($3,313 or $584 plus $2,729 institutional or foundational) and the Boomers third ($2,914 or $104 outright plus $2,810 institutional or foundational).

Boomers may eventually produce more outright gifts as they pay off their debt and move into what will be a more spartan older existence than the one both GIs and Silents experience. But what is important here is to understand the ratio of outright gifts and institutional gifts for each generation. Of this total gift history, GIs produce 38.8 percent outright gifts and 61.2 percent institutional gifts. For the Silent Generation, the figures are 17.6 percent outright and 82.4 percent institutional. Boomers come in at 3.6 percent outright and 96.4 percent institutional. It is no wonder that in Chapter Three of this volume Barry Kosmin reflects so well on concern about Jewish Boomer attitudes toward traditional federated appeals: this concern is shared by all federated agencies.

I suggest that each practitioner conduct this kind of analysis of his or her board in order to understand the theories behind generational archetypes and the cultures behind particular generations. Doing so will also help reveal just how the generational mix of a particular board and donor base suggests where a development office should place itself in its marketing campaigns both now and in the future. For instance, a typical response to a board with heavy GI leadership suggests not only a major gifts campaign but a planned giving campaign as well. A donor base with a large Silent Generation contingency might look forward to a charitable gift annuity vehicle. A Boomer board might be motivated through teamwork to acquire large government or foundation grants. It is as important for the fundraising professional to engage in intergenerational team building on any project or drive as it is to engage in interethnic team building.

Failure to understand the generational mix of one's board or donor base can lead to feelings of the kind expressed by a wealthy GI widow who, after dedicating years of work to her church, is now withholding her gifts and removing her church from her will: "They [the Boomers] are just piddling away the money our generation worked so hard to endow that church with."

It is not that this woman is not dedicated or generous. It is rather that the minister and lay leaders of the church have failed to recognize and understand her values and to connect them with those of the Boomers. Money that could have gone with the widow's enthusiastic support to endow a Sunday School curriculum will now go instead to this GI's alma mater to ensure a perpetual scholarship. The university was smart enough to send a representative of the Silent Generation, who listened to her. In contrast, the Boomer minister was interested only in telling the GI why spending the endowments from her friends' and relatives' estates was the morally correct thing to do. Thus the practitioner needs to ask not only how he or she sees other generational cultures but how members of those cultures see the practitioner.

Assimilation of new arrivals to new generational archetypes

For newly arrived immigrant groups, generational cultures may eventually exercise more influence than the ethnic culture does. For instance, in Miami the Cuban community has an economic enclave in which it is possible to do business without speaking English or ever dealing with a native American. Nonetheless, Generation X Cubans, as they move into marketing and financial positions in regional and multinational corporations, resemble other Generation Xers. They are willing to work on the projects that are necessary to meet United Way goals for their corporation.

Perhaps one of the most dramatic understandings of acculturation to generational cycles can be found in the Haitian community in Miami. It is impossible for those not familiar with Haitian culture to understand how truly foreign that experience is compared with the predominant culture in the United States. In a piece on Haiti, the "McNeil-Lehrer News Hour" (Aug. 24, 1994) explained that the country is 90 percent Roman Catholic and 100 percent Voodoo. Yet Protestant churches abound in the Little Haiti section of Miami; in fact, 40 percent of the Haitians living in Miami are Protestant.

Preliminary (and as yet unpublished) research by Frantz Jean-Louis (Visiting Program Director, Center for Labor Research and Studies, Florida International University) indicates the reason for this phenomenon. It is not that more Protestants moved to Miami from Haiti but rather that more became Protestant after they moved. These people view the Protestant church as a bridge to the United States. As with most immigrant churches, Haitian churches experience higher attendance and more dedicated giving than those of other indigenous ethnicities. What is most revealing about Jean-Louis's research for our purposes is that it demonstrates too the rate at which Haitians are assimilating not only to the dominant culture but also to the dominant culture's generational cycles.

Although he was unaware of the Strauss and Howe book until after completing the research on his community, Jean-Louis described four basic demographic groups. A group of 35- to 55-year-olds (Boomer age) were the first immigrants. They are becoming increasingly bitter and depressed as they are being estranged from their 18 to 25 year old (Generation X) children who are already acculturated to the new environment. A later immigration wave made up of 25 to 35 year olds (also Generation Xers) have not become as acculturated as the 18 to 25 year olds but certainly do not feel "out of it." And their offspring, Millennials, will be both totally acculturated and specifically Civic in their desire to build institutions for Haitians and the larger community alike.

Using this example, where can the fundraiser look for philanthropy in this community? Simple statistical analysis might suggest going to the churches for support. But more sophisticated generational analysis will tell us that the churches will need counseling programs for the depressed Boomer cohort. U.S. Boomers can reach out to their compatriots from this other culture. With each passing year, Haitian money to support these programs will be found in increasing amounts from age 35 down. Generation X Haitians will support such programs almost on a one-to-one basis, giving because they know someone close who was helped by a program. Young Haitian Millennials may build the institutions to care for their aged great-aunts and great-uncles, who will be in their seventies and eighties.

Looking forward

Philanthropists today need to realize that among the best-positioned organizations for future growth is Habitat for Humanity, which uses Boomer hands to work toward easily understandable, readily accessible projects. Children's organizations are also well positioned for the next decade. Boomer projects generally will involve their ability to access government funds and private foundation money. Boomers will also be drawn to low-overhead movements.

While we "think globally and act locally," we will be doing fundraisers for children, the environment, and multicultural endeavors. We will push charitable annuity funds to the Silent Generation. But most of all, we will find that we must communicate. If the United States is to refrain from tearing itself apart as it reacts to the Boomers' (Idealist) diverse, highly moral arguments and insistence, it will need fundraiser-communicators who are able to tie the cause of children to that of the environment, of victory to quality of life, of spirituality to service, and of relief of suffering and starvation to motherhood. This may sound like an easy task but in a balkanized world, it is not.

The fundraising practitioner is a communicator—even a peacemaker—in one of the most important and exciting human exchanges, that between the donor and the organization as they come to agreement. But so many variables stand in the way of successfully completing any such exchange. I hope this brief excursion into the concept of generational archetypes has shown that generational differences are quite real and understandable and can be used to help the fundraising practice.

Reference

Strauss, W., and Howe, N. *Generations: The History of America's Future, 1584 to 2069.* New York: William Morrow, 1991.

CHARLES L. EASTMAN *is executive director of the United Protestant Appeal in Miami, Florida. Prior to that he served as minister of the First Church of North Miami.*

Index

25, 26, 29, 82–83, 90, 96, 97, 115,
116, 120
Tao Teh Chin, 56
Taoism, 56
Tax incentives, 13
Taylor, M., 72, 78
Television appeals, 31
"Tell Them We Are Rising" program,
17
Test, M. A., 115, 122
Tienda, M., 24, 38, 39
Tirado, A., 28, 38
Tobin, G. A., 43, 51
Tonai, R. M., 57, 63
Torres-Gil, F., 24, 39
Trust, 28, 30, 32
Tzedakah, 45

U-shaped curve, 82, 91–93, 94–95
Understanding function, 113, 117, 119
Unions, 36
United Jewish Appeal (JUA)/Federation
campaign, 42, 46, 47, 48
United Latino Fund, 32, 33–34
United Negro College Fund (UNCF),
15
United Way, 31, 32, 33, 34, 58
Upper-income households. *See* High-
income households
U.S. Bureau of the Census, 54, 86, 109
U.S. Congress, 24, 39
U.S. Department of Commerce, 24, 39
U.S. Department of Education, 24, 39

Valencia, H., 31, 39
Values, influence of. *See* Motivation;
Seven Faces framework
Values function, 113, 115, 119
Vest, J. L., 29, 39, 56, 58, 63
Vietnamese Americans, 60
Villarreal, J., 29, 39, 56, 58, 63
Volunteer Functions Inventory (VFI),
113–114, 118

Volunteerism: African American, 19;
connections of, to giving, 118, 120;
functional approach to, 112–114;
and Generation X archetype, 142;
Jewish, 45–46; motivations for,
111–114; psychological functions
of, 113–114
von Schlegell, A. J., 71–72, 78

Walker, C. J., 12
Watson, B. C., 20, 21
Wealth: African American, 16; and con-
tribution amount, 100, 101; and
fundraising, 107–108; versus in-
come, 98; measures of, 98, 100; and
income percentage contributed,
100, 101, 102; and participation
rate, 100, 101, 103–104; relationship of, to giving, 81, 98–105, 106–
107. *See also* Income level; Dynast
personality type; Major donors
Weisbrod, B. A., 126, 135
Weitzman, E., 43
Weitzman, M. S., 25, 38, 82, 108, 126,
134
White, R., 112, 123
Willmer, W., 3
Wills, G., 125, 135
Wind, Y., 125, 135
Winters, M. F., 21
Wolpert, J., 2–3
Women in philanthropy: in African
American philanthropy, 70;
fundraising implications of, 72–76;
in Jewish philanthropy, 47, 48,
49–50; motivations of, 71–72, 75;
philanthropic power of, 67–68, 70;
progressive influence of, 69–71;
and small donations, 70; upper-
class white, 69–71
Women of the Upper Class (Ostrander), 71
Woolley, J. M., 120, 123
Wuthnow, R., 126, 135

Ordering Information

NEW DIRECTIONS FOR PHILANTHROPIC FUNDRAISING is published quarterly in Fall, Winter, Spring, and Summer and is available for purchase by subscription and individually.

SUBSCRIPTIONS for 1994–95 cost $59.00 for individuals (a savings of 35 percent over single-copy prices) and $79.00 for institutions, agencies, and libraries. Please do not send institutional checks for personal subscriptions. Standing orders are accepted. For subscription sales outside of the United States, contact any international subscription agency or Jossey-Bass directly.

SINGLE COPIES cost $19.95 plus shipping (see below) when payment accompanies order. California, New Jersey, New York, and Washington, D.C., residents please include appropriate sales tax. Canadian residents add GST and any local taxes. Billed orders will be charged shipping and handling. No billed shipments to post office boxes. Orders from outside the United States and Canada *must be prepaid* in U.S. dollars or charged to VISA, MasterCard, or American Express.

SHIPPING (SINGLE COPIES ONLY): one issue, add $3.50; two issues, add $4.50; three issues, add $5.50; four to five issues, add $6.50; six to seven issues, add $7.50; eight or more issues, add $8.50.

DISCOUNTS for quantity orders are available. Please write to the address below for information.

ALL ORDERS must include either the name of an individual or an official purchase order number. Please submit your order as follows:
   Subscriptions: specify series and year subscription is to begin
   Single copies: include individual title code (such as PF1)

MAIL ALL ORDERS TO: Jossey-Bass Publishers, 350 Sansome Street, San Francisco, California 94104-1342.

Previous Issues Available